# DANCING
# TO
# SADIE

## Austin Gilroy

# DANCING TO SADIE

BY

## AUSTIN GILROY

BrightKing Publications
142 Devonshire Way,
Shirley,
Croydon,
Surrey CR0 8BT
England.

Telephone: 0208 777 3032
International: 00442087773032
Email: gilroycromcruach@hotmail.com

And

Munlough, Bawnboy, Co. Cavan,
EIRE.

ISSUED BY:
BrightKing Publications
142 Devonshire Way
Shirley
Croydon
Surrey
CR0 8BT
England

*And*

Munlough
Bawnboy
Co. Cavan
Eire.

To Agnes
with love

Custin + +

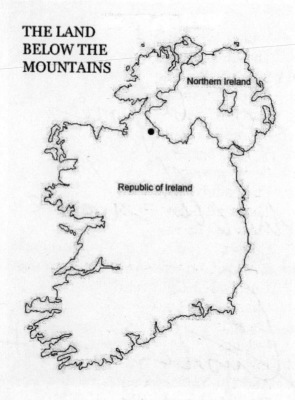

# THE LAND
# BELOW THE
# MOUNTAINS

Northern Ireland

Republic of Ireland

# Contents

# 1

## *Winter Wonderland.*

My God this was absolutely marvellous. I was standing near the Sally Park Gap watching the snowflakes zigzagging crazily from the sky. The advance guards were wiped out, melted by whatever warmth remained in the earth, but their reinforcements, pouring downwards in ever increasing numbers established a bridgehead and then secured the territory-this was wonderful-but would it last? Would it snow all night leaving a blanket a foot deep on the ground by morning?

I was so happy. The sky was scattering the snow on the house and farm in Teeboy. With gentle care it covered every blade of grass, every rock, bush and tree in sight. Nothing escaped its white generosity, not a crack or a crevice. The whiteness cured all imperfections, every wrinkle and age line was smoothed over, and our parish was reborn once more in its baptismal robe of purity.

My brothers and sisters were already pelting each other with lumps of it while screaming and yelling with a mixture of delight and feigned terror. But the snow kept coming down, silently wrapping with clinical efficiency all in its path with an ever fatter mantle of joy. Within an hour a four-foot tall snowman complete with eyes, ears, nose and pipe-in-mouth was standing proudly beside our door.

It was the day before Christmas Eve and the countryside was now bathed in a glow of light, surreal and beautiful.

The lake being already frozen over, the snow settled on its vast expanse and completed the unbroken veil of white from the Cuilcagh mountains to the far horizon.

Of course the presence of the snow was not welcomed by everyone. The cattle had to be given a lot more care. My Father and

Frank had to carry buckets of water from the gravel hole to their stalls in the byre, and each cow could drink a couple of buckets. Later on they carried hay in loads tied by ropes on their backs to the "dry" cattle in the outlying fields...but the present exhilaration belonged to us, and we savoured it to the full, extracting every last ounce of happiness and excitement from our winter visitor.

A couple of pieces of wood nailed together and pulled by string was our idea of a toboggan, or rather our invention of the object having never seen or heard of one before. One of us sat on it holding on for dear life while two others ran, one on each side, pulling the strings and building up as fast a speed as possible, before releasing the willing victim to an almost certain crash into a thorny quick halfway down the lane. But whether bloodied or bruised you got up, shook off the snow, pulled out the thorns and brought the toboggan back up for the next rider to have a go.

This was a kind of rehearsal or matinee for the main event, when we could arrange a combined session with our neighbouring children the McGoverns, Smiths, Byrnes and Priors or on a larger scale the first day back at school...but that would have to wait.

The light faded around five o'clock and Mama called us in for tea - hot strips of bacon between thick slices of home made bread, baked in the oven over the open fire, and mugs of tea. My father filled the oil lamp, lit the two wicks, put on the globe and hung it from the "S" hook near the window. Then we settled down at the table, playing cards, ludo, snakes & ladders or draughts, while Mama and Dada sat near the fire and exchanged some of their hopes, fears, triumphs and disappointments in tones mellowed by years of mutual contentment and accommodation.

The "stirabout" or porridge was handed round about ten o'clock, before we said our prayers and went up the stairs to bed. We were tingling with excitement and anticipation because tomorrow...Christmas Eve was going to be a magical and exhausting day!


"Get up! Get up!"

Pulling the clothes off Enda and Frank's bed the moment I awoke - only waiting to look out the window and make sure that God had answered my prayers and he had...the snow was still

2

THE CROSS AT THE SPRING. THE RALLYING POINT FOR "HUNTING THE WRAN".

there. it was almost a foot deep.

A hurried breakfast over and we were trying to catch the donkey. My father would still not allow us to bring the horse and cart on our own, so we were reduced to the second division of transport, the donkey and cart. Looking back I think this was even more dangerous as the donkey being a stallion certainly had a mind of his own!

Eventually we rattled off on the iron wheeled cart, down past "Neds" and up "Jim Micks" hill to Feehans, our first port of call.

The shop was full of everything that a typical family in the area regarded as essential; tea, sugar, bread, butter, cakes, fig roll biscuits, jam, ham, custards and jellies to name but a few. A large barrel in the middle of the floor was full of salted herrings and the walls sported spades, shovels, pitchforks, grapes, and Wellington boots in all sizes but only one colour.

Feehans street was chock full of transport...bicycles, donkeys and carts, horses and traps and even a couple of ford Prefects. The clientele were insisting on dragging their very willing neighbours into the pub at the back of the shop for "one for the Christmas"; "Its seldom we meet you out" they choroused; and there were many shouts of "Happy Christmas", and "I hope the next year will be good one", and "Isn't it a shame oul Mickey isn't with us any longer", and "a decenter man you could not meet".

Feehans was buzzing with the men and women from the small farms of Corlough and they were being rewarded for their years patronage with free jugs of stout and large hot whiskeys and port for the ladies, but we being underage these delicacies were still forbidden fruit and we were feasting instead on lemonade and biscuits and Cavan Cola.

We had a long list of goods drawn up by Mama to purchase and we were given gifts of tea, sugar and cake by the generous shopkeepers. All purchases were wrapped in brown paper and tied with twine from the ball hanging by the counter and amidst many shouted good wishes and cries of "see you at midnight mass", or "are you going burying the 'wran'", and now being the richer by numerous brown threepenny bits and silver sixpences, we extricated our chuckwagon and donkey and beat a steady tattoo down towards Phil Thomas's cross and on to Devine's cross where we turned right, right again and left to Cassidy's shop.

Cassidys was located at the edge of the lough, just beyond the sandpit and past the yew tree, which stood at the site where Arderra chapel had been in days gone by. You were always sure of a warm welcome at Cassidys.

The shop itself was located in the room on the left as you went in the door of the dwelling house and the rows of sweets in tins on the top shelf was a sight for sore eyes. A large weighing scale stood on one end of the counter and in the drawers on the left the tobacco was kept...Warrior Plug and Yachtmans...sold by the ounce or half quarter and cut by a sharp knife attached to a flat piece of wood. It was in Cassidys that I first heard a radio - the programme was "Dan Dare, Pilot of the future". Normally we would travel to Cassidys by bicycle or on foot along the Arderra lane, which entailed going down past Neds, turning right at the cross of the spring, on past the fairy fort, past Arthurs, Gregorys, and past the entrance to the former Arderra School, where tradition maintained a ghost...a lady in white...searching for her lost lover frequently appeared, and to the yew tree cross as before.

Not so today. It being Christmas Eve we were really doing the rounds. I suppose you could call it our version of "Shop till you drop"-- so when we left Cassidys we turned in the opposite direction and meandered along Lakefield road, past the lakes and homes of Owens, Donoughues, Dolans and Plunketts to Smiths of the Cross where we turned left for Bawnboy or Bawn as we called it.

We tied the donkey outside Mullallys, which was another shop and public house combined, and there we completed our purchases of the Christmas essentials with some sweets and goodies from McGeoughs or the Millers with any drapery items from Darcys or Nellie Flynns.

The winter days being now at their shortest, darkness was almost upon us, so seating ourselves snugly in the hay between the groceries we turned our steps or rather the donkey's steps towards Teeboy. With no lights whatsoever our dark little chuck wagon trudged homewards but those were the days before cars had taken a grip on our paradise and all you were likely to meet was another donkey and cart, pedestrians or a cyclist most likely also travelling without a light.

By the time we got home the stuffed turkey was sitting on the table awaiting its appointment with the oven and my mother and Noelle were putting up pieces of holly in the kitchen which was also of course our living room. Enda was up in Aunt Maggies as she didn't like to stay on her own and needed, as she put it "someone young and able to run for help if needed". Frank and myself immediately sat down to a meal of bacon, eggs, sausages and a special treat of fried slices of boxty, which was only made twice a year...at Halloween and Christmas. The moment Frank finished his tea he had to go up the nearway, over the fields to Aunt Maggies to let Enda come home as he was going to Midnight Mass with the rest of us.

Father had already fothered the animals, milked any cows still milking at this time of year, and settled them down for the night.

Dolly, as our horse was somewhat ambiguously called, had a bit of special treatment. He sported a nosebag over his head in his stable with a measure of his favourite food....oats, and a coat on his back, an overbright creation which had arrived from America as a kind of private version of Marshall aid, and which neither want, desperation nor threats could force anyone to wear. Dolly would need all his strength to pull the trap and its occupants up the hills to Corlough chapel in time for the midnight devotions.

Christmas Eve was always the highlight of the festive season for us. The excitement and anticipation it generated were unmatched by any other event of the year, religious or secular.

At the time I am writing of, my brothers Frank, Enda and sister Noelle and myself were living at home with our parents. Our eldest brother Paddy and sister Rita (or Etta as we called her) were living and working in Dublin and Tony was in Loughrea in Galway, but all of them were coming home for Christmas. We were very excited, waiting for them to arrive and every couple of minutes, Mama or one of us would go out and listen to hear if Neds dog was barking, as that would be a sure sign that they were coming up the road.

About nine o'clock they arrived with presents of

CORLOUGH CHAPEL.

Sandeman sherry, Warrior Plug tobacco, chocolates, cakes and sweets. They had made marathon trips, first of all by bus to Cavan, another bus to Bawn and then any lift they could get from there. As cars were so few and far between you were nearly guaranteed to have to walk or as stated in the local vernacular use "Shanks Mare" for the last couple of miles.

Tony had managed to get a lift with "little Joe" the undertaker and emerged from the back of the hearse in the darkness on the street to the consternation of my mother.

Great were the welcomes back to the bosom of the family, my mother fussing and hugging them, admiring bonnets and suits, thanking them for their gifts while we hovered around hoping for a shilling or two to swell our coffers.

Enda was now helping Father to tackle Dolly into his trap. Meanwhile the curtains were pulled aside to prevent fire and a candle was lit in every window. Two lighted candles were also placed in our trap lamps-one on each side, and finally having lit his pipe with a burning coal from the fire, held in the metal tongs, father gathered us into the trap and we set off.

**Corlough was a magical sight.**

Candles glittered in the windows of every house dotted along the hills, and the moon and stars answered back casting a welcome benevolent glow over the countryside, as the faithful wended their way to celebrate Christ's birth together.

It was a scene that had not changed in almost one hundred and fifty years, ever since Catholic Emancipation had enabled us to worship God in the way we desired. There was a procession of horses and traps, some people walking and others on bikes, all making their way over to Devines cross and up past Tonlegee hall. When we arrived at the Chapel, we loosened the horse from the trap and tied him in one of the arches underneath the building.

It was pure theatre, a pageant, with each one playing a prominent role.

The chapel was cold at first and lit by oil lamps but the press and closeness of six or seven hundred people soon warmed it. Enda and myself were two of the servers, in total seven or eight, one to take the mass book from one side to the other, one to ring the bell hopefully at the appointed times, one to hold the paten during communion, one or two to light the candles on the altar and two to take up the collection. I was a member of the latter duo and unfortunately owing to my position on the altar, drew the short straw. You see the boxes were on the ends of long handles which extended to about four or five feet in length and when these were gradually filled up with copper and silver, the heavier one would have required, at the very least, a budding Charles Atlas, to manoeuvre it safely over the heads of the parishioners.

My fellow collector who was positioned on the side of the altar nearest the sacristy was in like a hare when the appointed time came and secured the lighter box and I was left with the hammer of Thor. Now the collection was done in a strict routine. We started on the men's side. Yes our church had men on the right and women on the left and the first collection area was the small section near the confession box on the right hand side, and having safely negotiated round there, we then proceeded down the main right hand side lifting the boxes over the mens' heads from front to back. The boxes were gradually getting heavier, filling up with anything from the large old pennies featuring the hen and chickens, to sixpences, two-shilling pieces or even half-crowns.

As you got nearer the back, where most of the latchikoes hung out, things became more difficult. Some of them might hold the box just to annoy you or maybe put in an odd stone, or a nail or anything they had to hand. Occasionally a kinder soul might put in a couple of sweets, which you could have for yourself.

By this time the boxes and especially, the hammer of Thor, was very heavy indeed, and now my colleague and I moved over to the women's side. As his box was a good bit lighter in itself he was able to maintain a dignified progress and I had to proceed as best I could, knocking off hats, destroying beehive haircuts and giving not inconsiderable bumps on the backs of heads as my weary arms endeavoured to lift the box up and down continuously on my journey to the front.

But this was only a side show to the real event...the choir sang the hymns:

"Hark the Herald Angels Sing";
"Star of Bethlehem";

"Adeste Fidelis";  and
"Silent Night".

We answered the Latin responses...The Priest beginning "AD DEUM QUE LAETIFICAT JUVEN TUTUM MEUM" and we replied "QUE TO EUS DEUS FORTITUDE MEAM", Father Brady gave his homily, Holy Communion was distributed, the Last Gospel was said, yes there was a Last Gospel in those days, and the service ended.

We journeyed home in the horses and traps, under the starry sky, amongst our friends and neighbours, in a scene which could have been enacted in any century from the eighth to the twentieth, but has now in the space of a few short years vanished from the landscape.

I didn't sleep that night waiting to see what Santa Claus had left, in the longest sock I could find and which I hung carefully on the crook in the fireplace.

Christmas day itself was a lazy fat day compared to Christmas Eve. Lashings of turkey, potatoes, peas, carrots, cabbage and gravy, followed by jelly and custard, tea and cakes were consumed.

It was our midwinter Saturnalian feast. Sherry or Port for the ladies, Whiskey and bottles of Guinness for the men, and Cavan Cola and Lemonade for us youngsters. None of us went out visiting on that day. It was for family renewal and a bit of excess. No matter how good or how bad the year had been Christmas day was much the same as much of everything as you wanted...not indeed that our wants were many. We were easily satisfied. Our greedy instincts had not been whetted up to a fine appetite by the advertising manipulation, which is prevalent today. An India rubber ball, an orange, a toy gun or a bow and arrow, a doll or a teddy bear was quite enough for the children of that era.

The next day (St. Stephens, or Boxing Day) was quite different. It was a day of constant activity and in spite of its saintly connections we hankered back to something more ancient long before St. Stephen had ever been heard of, to before the era of recorded time. We had just celebrated the Christian feast of Christmas and now we turned to a memory of our pagan

THE ARCHES BENEATH THE CHAPEL
WHERE THE HORSES WERE TETHERED.

past..."Hunting the Wran".

The wren has many mythological connections in Celtic folklore, all of which were completely unknown to us, but yet the memory survived in the tribe's subconsciousness. Of course what we enjoyed was the companionship of our friends, the cakes and lemonade and naturally the money we would gather as we wound our way around the lower half of the parish.

Our assembly point was the "Cross of the Spring" at eleven o'clock. Three of the Priors were there - Cathal, Brendan and Cyril, Paddy Smith, Aidan Byrne and Enda and myself, dressed in stout boots, Fairisle jumpers and jackets complete with woollen hats and scarves and each disguised by a mask, cut I think from Kelloggs corn flake boxes and depicting Red Indian chiefs.

We were all well acquainted with our plan of action...each had a tin whistle or mouth organ and although none of us was a great musician or dancer, nevertheless that was the fare that was going to be on offer. I know for a fact that none of us could play a note on the tin whistle or mouth organ and certainly had not mastered the art of dancing but musical or dancing talent was not a prerequisite for membership of our Corlough Light Orchestra. No, what was absolutely necessary was to have the lungs to enable you to blow the instruments as loudly as possible whilst moving your fingers furiously over the holes as if you had an idea which notes you were going to produce, and not just random noises while some of the troupe danced around like whirling dervishes which was as near as we got to the statuesque art of dancing!

We set off through upper Teeboy, calling at Artie Atties (Devines), John Darcys, Duffys, James and Joe Priors, Paddy Connors, John James and Red Pat Martins, John Reillys, Dolans, McGoverns, Tommy Farrelys...in fact all round through Cuiliagh, then over to Bonebroke to both the Reilly Houses, Donoughies and every other house on the way.

We were brought in to each house and invited to play and dance on the stone floors, while our hosts tried to guess our names, as they had a very good idea of our overall group but our disguise made individual identification difficult. They plied us with Christmas goodies, tried to get a better look at us as we ate them, and put coins in our collection box.

In the evening, getting ever more tired, and more plump by each household we turned homeward through Cortoon calling at Michael Oliver Foxs and past Feehans pub where the patrons greatly increased our assets. We reached our original starting point...the cross at the spring. Pee McGoverns (Neds) was the nearest house to the cross and here we converged and made it our last port of call.

There was a very good reason for this. Neds house was within easy reach for all of us and all the children in the family were girls. In those pre-womens lib days only boys went out "Burying the Wran" so the house was of course a neutral venue for the division of our newly acquired wealth.

The loot was arranged into piles of halfcrowns, florins, schillings, sixpences, threepenny bits, twopenny, penny and halfpenny pieces and divided equally between us with any left over halfpennies being tossed for, so after a few calls of heads or harp (We never said tails) all was sorted out.

After more tea and cake we headed for home with our now individual treasuries, a grand amount of seven shillings and sixpence each as I recall from my last trip, weighing us down in the receptive snow.

## 2

# *The Awakening.*

The Seasons and weather governed our lives and we paid reverential homage to any sign or person who could give an iota of an inkling as to what was in store.

If the crows flew home early one evening someone would remark, "Ah, that will surely mean rain". If a crane flew from the lake towards the mountain the forecast was equally bad but brighter times were on the way if the crane was flying the opposite way. For the immediate outlook we reckoned rain wasn't far away if the wind was blowing from the direction of Ballinamore but you wouldn't need a raincoat if it was blowing towards the small Leitrim town.

The years work started with a trip to Frank Cafferty's forge in Dermodys lane to get Dolly a new set of shoes.

A forge has the honour of being the oldest workshop in the world and has retained the same formula since metals and in particular iron was first smelted. It's shape, equipment and smells would have been very familiar to the Celts of the Iron Age. The aroma, a mixture of horse manure and scorched hoofs, as red hot shoes are tried for fit, would have been just the same on the Anatolian plains where Celtic horsemen overwhelmed their enemies and on their journeys right across Europe to their sea bound kingdom on the western shore.

It is small wonder that blacksmiths were renowned in Celtic mythology and to a people with a consuming love of horses, the man who fashioned their shoes, who gave flight to their wings, was a mighty man indeed.
The forge would be full, six or seven men watching the blacksmith shoe a horse while their own were tethered outside waiting their

turn. He would remove the old worn shoes, trim the hooves with a sharp curved knife and try on shoes that would be reddening in his bellows driven fire. Adjustments were made by hammering the shoe while holding it over the neck of the anvil before nailing it to the hoof with seven nails. Then a final trim of the hoof with the knife and any imperfections were filed down with the rasp.

It was a marvellous day bringing the horse to the forge and listening to the craic but it was a completely different matter when I had to bring the donkey. First of all nobody else would bring him because he was a stallion who didn't like the smithy...and the feeling was mutual. The donkey would have very long hooves which needed a lot of trimming and he would often yank his head around and try or maybe succeed in biting the smithy who would instantly retaliate. I would be very relieved when the job was done and I could canter down the lane homewards and not have to undergo that ordeal for another year.

With the horse shod and any running repairs to the plough, cart and harness out of the way, we were ready for the off. We reluctantly emerged from the semi hibernation of winter to the vitality of spring. Its coming was announced by the snowdrops and the buds on the branches and the vibrant green cloak which the fields were busily arraying themselves in.

Spring did not rely solely on a visual display. It had a soundtrack as well and a panoramic one at that...a thousand voice choir by our feathered neighbours from the wren, blackbird and thrush to the humming of the wood pigeon and the non melodic efforts of the crow. Occasionally winter's rearguard tried to creep back and scouting forays of wind and sleet or even snow showers attempted to reclaim the territory it had lost, to no avail. The sun, the tangible evidence of God, was on his journey Northwards and his all powerful life-force was renewing creation and directing the course of our labours as assuredly as any manager or director in factory or office. It had nothing to do with the automated soul destroying set up of a production line. It wasn't trying to squeeze another percentage of profit out of human beings or in the words of Henry Ford seeing just how elastic they were.

Our God, through his Sun was restarting his endless cycle to feed and nourish all the living things of his creation and the first item we knew we had to do was the ploughing.

Scores of seagulls followed the plough, as under father's grip and the horse's strength the blade turned the sod and exposed thousands of worms, grubs and insects, some of whom were devoured as a gastronomic delight to partly soothe the voracious appetite of the air force army swooping from on high. Ploughing was a very strenuous task for man and beast or more truly men and beasts because it needed more that one of each species to plough virgin or lea ground. Most farmers only had one horse so a system of "cooring" operated whereby two farmers combined and harnessed both their horses to the plough and while one held the plough handles the other would drive the horses and stand or jump on the overturned sod to ensure it did not fall back down to its original position. The lines had already been marked out and manure spread so the two sods formed a ridge with the manure inside to await the seed potatoes.

Sometimes we bought new seed..."Donegal Certified" was the most popular but more often we used some of the best potatoes from the previous years crop. These had been cut into halves or thirds to make the seed, providing they each had a good clear "eye" from which the new shoots would emerge and feed on the old piece of potato for its initial sustenance. The holes for the seeds were made by a stick called a "stieviin" with an edge halfway between being rounded and pointed, and a wedge about seven or eight inches from the end which allowed the holder to exert pressure with his foot and make the hole. The hole maker was followed by a youngster - the "guggerer", with a bucket of seeds, one of which he inserted in each hole with hopefully the eye as upwards as possible. The hole was then closed by the "stieviin" man and we awaited the miracle to happen with boundless confidence. The seeds were sprinkled with lime before setting to discourage predatory slugs or other chancers who might be lurking with intentions of a free meal.

When the stalks were about three or four inches high we scored the furrows with the plough and shovelled the mould over and around the stalks to give them extra strength, and a few weeks later we journeyed along each ridge pulling up by hand all and any weeds which had dared to flaunt themselves. Another preventative

THE FORMER HOLY TRINITY CHURCH, KILDOAGH.
- A BARN TYPE CHURCH, SITE OF DEVOTIONS TO
ST. MOGUE. THE CLAY FROM AROUND THIS CHURCH
IS REPUTED TO SAFEGUARD AGAINST FIRE AND
STORMS AND WAS CARRIED BY A SURVIVOR OF
THE TITANIC DISASTER.

measure employed when the stalks were quite high was to spray them with a water and bluestone solution. The solution was carried in a container...a sprayer on our backs which we pumped with one hand and directed the spray through a nozzle on the end of a piece of tubing held in the other hand. The aim of this operation was to prevent the dreaded blight...and no Irishman needed to be reminded of the devastating effects an infestation of this disease could cause. Its history had left an indelible mark, never to be erased.

Older generations did not have the use of the plough and some still dug the lea ground with Loys - a truly enormous spade-like instrument which at that time I was barely able to lift. I tell you, you had to be a real man to work a Loy. My grandfather used one for all his digging. He also had a special tip of his own to ensure a successful crop. When the stalks were a few inches high, just before the moulding, he laid lightly twisted hay ropes in the furrows between the ridges and burned them. The idea was to deal a deathly blow to the dreaded slugs who might be massing for an attack but there might be a vestige of the reverence for the purifying effect of fire.

The penitential period of Lent occurs during this time and we often gave up sweets or maybe the men might give up drink as our contribution, but it would be too long a time for the fun loving Celts to adhere strictly and we had our safety valve. Right there in the middle we had our own Bacchanalian festival - St. Patrick's Day. We prayed to our national apostle and played football in the snow-free hills. We had given up eating sweets for Lent but we still accepted any offered to us and saved them for this day of dispensation, when we could gorge ourselves with full ecclesiastical licence.

Spirits were high and manufactured spirits were lowered without difficulty and The Mountain Road pipe and drum band marched through Ballyconnell, and in the evening the older teenagers and those still 'going out' or unattached went to the Ceili and Old time in Tonlegee or the more modern fare which in later years was on offer in the Star or Wonderland.

Many were the headaches the following day but memories were stored away to bring a smile or a tear in years to come to many, some still in the Emerald Isle and some in cities the world over. A sense of propriety and abstinence descended again for the remainder of Lent to be finally dissipated by the exuberance of Easter.

Before Easter arrived the potatoes would have been joined in their incubation by our other staples, cabbage, turnips, onions, rhubarb, carrots and oats to wait an Irish harvest day.

A whole new pastime opened up at this time of the year...fishing. trout, perch, roach, bream and pike, with a few hybrids thrown in. The purists divide them into Trout fishing and others which they classify as course fishing, but we lumped them all together and our equipment was exactly the same. A strong hazel rod cut from the gurteen or Priors glen and a line and hook bought from Coulstons in Ballyconnell with a cork for a float.

Many happy hours were spent testing the possibilities at the Black Banks or Hoynss and Gregorys shore where a battery of stones had been built to allow us to go out further into the lake to avail of the deeper water, or further afield at Feehans river, the Blackwater, Glencourthna or Port Lake.

Now and then we might row the boat for Peter the Baker who was one armed and who loved to trawl for pike, and then one or two would get the chance to transverse the whole of Ardara lake. The greatest sacrilege was get your line entangled with that of a fellow fisher and it was nearly as bad to get it caught in a branch of the overhanging trees at the Black Banks. Either misfortune meant spending ages trying to untangle the resultant Gordion's knot and nobody would be too happy at the thought of fishing next to you again.

The most hair-raising part was gingerly negotiating your way homewards through the ancient bog holes and shaking scraws from the Black Banks, carrying any fish we had captured on forked branches passed through their gills and mouths. Fishing in the Spring was however a hit and miss affair as our quarry were too lethargic owing to the coldness of the water, and it was later in the warmer evenings when we were most successful, or so the experts on the subject often proclaimed.

Lent was inclined to drag on a bit, with no pictures (we never said films), being shown in the "Star", no dances or Ceilis, no card playing, no sweets and additional devotions on a Friday evening. To cap it all on certain days, you were only supposed to eat "one meal and two collations", but as far as I remember we ate whatever was available without any qualms. It's a wonder Lent caught on at all.

But at last Easter Sunday dawned, and the gloom of abstinence, so alien to the spirit of the Celt, lifted from our hills and glens and we eagerly reached for the life force again.

After Mass we quickly ate our dinner and set out for the football match and our yearly outdoor picnic on Priors hill. We had very few chocolate Easter eggs but plenty of the good old hen manufactured variety, which we boiled on fires of sticks overlooking the fairy glen and after the football, finished off the evening with a fishing trip to the Black Banks.

We celebrated the feast of "Bealtaine" on the eve of the first of May. This was nothing to do with the church and was not officially recognised in any way, but had remained doggedly in the folk memory from millennia before St. Patrick had ever visited our shores. It was a relic of our pagan Celtic heritage, which no amount of disapproval, or when that did not work, benign neglect, could eradicate.

A massive bonfire of whins, bushes and old hay or straw was set up and burned. Some people drove their cattle around it, "ar deisceall", or clockwise, and some drove them through kind of goalposts which had been lighted. Embers from the fire were thrown into fields of crops, especially the oats and potato fields, to ensure good luck and a bountiful harvest.

Nobody ever said publicly in whose honour this was being done but the site of the hump backed one, "Crom" was not very far away in Templeport.

# 3

## *Summer Breezes.*

Summer was a busy and magical time. It was the time of hay...cutting it, saving it and building it. The turf - the fuel for our everlasting fire, had to be cut and saved as well and brought home to the safety of the turfshed. And a plentiful supply of wood both heavy and light was required to supplement the turf.

We were called early on the Saturday morning - "Get up quick , we'll start the hay today ". We breakfasted quickly and then went down the field to catch Dolly. Sometimes he could be skittish and amble around just far enough out of reach to maintain his freedom but today the lure of oats in a bucket proved irresistible, and Dolly was captured for a days work. He was dressed out in his working gear - his burnished armoury of leather and brass and fitted into the shafts of the Deering moving machine. The Deering was a lighter machine than the Pierce and could be drawn by one horse, but two were usually required for the Pierce.

All the auguries had been consulted on the weather front - the cranes, the crows and finally the clincher - the long range forecast on Radio Eireann. Even still, nervous glances were cast in the direction of Ballinamore and tufts of grass tossed in the air to ensure that the fickle wind had not changed its direction.

The blade holder was lowered and the sharpened and oiled blade inserted, carefully attached to the ball of the revolving arm and we were ready for the off.

Carefully the first swathe was cut and raked out - "taking out the back swathe " as it was known in the trade , to prepare the way for the final swathe which would be mown last in the opposite direction after all the hay inside the area bounded by the first cut had been mown. After ten or so rounds of the meadow a stop was made to have a satisfying drink from the gallon of buttermilk, carefully positioned, out of harms way in a corner, although tiny frogs now and then jumped into it, whether by accident or desire, but these were just scooped out and by no means was the buttermilk wasted.

The hay was tedded on the Monday, apart from the fact that it was not usual to work on the Sunday, except in an emergency, it was considered good to leave the hay for a day to let the sun "kill" it. But come Monday morning it was all hands to the deck and the swathes were tedded, that is shook up with a pitchfork, and later rowed with a rake. "Rake with the grain" - the direction in which it was mowed, we were always told because if that was possible it was much easier. If the weather was really sunny and dry and preferably had a bit of a drying wind with it then our luck was in and by Tuesday night, the 'big meadow' which provided the bulk of the hay would be safely gathered up in cocks or winds, and these would be secured with hay ropes wound with a twister - a piece of bullwire fashioned for the job.

We had to make the most of the good weather when it came - literally we made hay while the sun shone - and so there were no trips back to the house for meals. These were brought out to us in the meadow by Mama or Noelle or Rita and food never tasted so good. Bread , butter and Jam , sometimes bacon and potatoes and plenty of tea in an enormous metal teapot or even a gallon and a couple of hard boiled eggs for each worker.

If the weather held good, then while we were winning one meadow Father would be mowing another and the process continued until all were won. But more likely than not the weather would break, as even the most respected of oracles have their off days, and we would have to wait and hope for an improvement before tackling the next lot. The worst scenario was when the weather, or Zeus started playing games with us, laughing from on high and only provided short periods that were dry enough for working and we had to resort to "lapping", small rolls wound into a circle to let the wind whistle underneath or "handshakings" and then wait to win them further before building them into cocks or winds.

I still remember the delicious taste of the honey we often

found in the wild bees nests in mossy areas of the meadows while winning the hay.

The turf cutting took place around the same time. It was very hard work but had the air of an outing - in fact each day was an outing in itself.

We had some turf on the moor but it was only sods suitable for the back of the fire, and even when placed there the "small white stones in those sods would take the eyes out of your head" as mother lamented, and she was right. When the sods were burning, the stones seemed to acquire the power of unaided flight, and could send many a one warming themselves too close to the fire scurrying for safer quarters a good bit away.

So we went further afield for our turf cutting and leased banks for the season in different places - Roberts bog above Corlough chapel, Hughie Edward Currans in Lannanaria before we and our neighbours obtained banks in Commas bog when the Land Commission divided it up. All three had different atmospheres but all had one thing in common - they were all very much uphill, and it was a good part of the days labour to get to them in the first place.

It was no use going to the bog without a good sharp slean and a wheelbarrow, preferably one with a wide wheel, and both had to be tied to a bicycle for the uphill trip. The slean fitted neatly along the crossbar but the wheelbarrow, and it was of the large variety, had to be tied on the back. The slean was a spade with a wing on one side of the blade and was sharpened with a long file, and when properly sharp and wielded by an expert could cut through the turf like butter.

The first bog I can recall was Hughie Edward Currans in Lannanaria. It was the last house before the mountain and there was a lovely waterfall on the river which flowed by it and near the bank was a dipping tank for sheep. Some years later we cut turf in Roberts bog and we left our bicycles at Reillys and walked across the hill. Hugh Cuffey, a great character, had the bank next to ours. The first time I went to Roberts bog I was home from College, and Enda for some reason wasn't coming that day, so I left my bicycle at Reillys as instructed, and set off over the hill. I couldn't believe my eyes. The man on the next bank had seen me and obviously thinking I was Enda, whom he knew well , had started dancing about and then standing on his head and walking on his hands. Nobody had told me about Hugh, so I didn't know what to make of the whole thing, but when he saw that I wasn't Enda he stopped his shenanagins and started working at a mile a minute, furiously spreading the turf as if his very life depended on it.

With a nod I started working as well, and there was great decorum for an hour or two. Eventually Hugh came over and when he found out that I was Enda's brother the craic soon started all over. He had a multitude of stories and was a very happy man and a hard worker , but he religiously broke off at noon and set off on his bicycle and cycled down to Bawn where he had a pint and a whisky and then up to Feehans for the same before returning to the bog. You see he had been a cook in the American army during the war and now had a pension which ensured he could indulge his tastes as he liked.

Now and then we didn't leave the bicycles at Reillys but continued up the road and came into the bog past Roberts house where I recall having the strongest and hottest panjur of tea in my life made by "Old Tom".

The trip to Commas was much longer and harder than to Roberts or even to Hughie Edwards bog. We cycled down to Dernacrieve, and turned left on the Glan road and started the climb up past Altachullion school to the Black Rocks, where stood the rock known as Maguires chair where it was said the Maguire chieftains were enthroned hundreds of years before. We turned right at the rocks and after a couple of miles turned left into the side road - another punishing hill, before the expanse of Commas lay before us. It had been nibbled at in tiny spots by intruding humans but remained largely the virgin territory it had always been since the last ice age. As I first viewed it a bank of cloud passed under the sun and a wave of colour moved rapidly from North to South. The colour changed each clump of heather, each wind shriven shrub, each hillock and valley. The colours were a moving panoramic kaleidoscope, a painter's brush being wielded by an unseen giant across a canvas of heather.

It was easy to imagine long dead liegemen of the Maguires, McGoverns, O'Rourkes, O'Reillys or indeed the O'Neills and

ARDARA LAKE - OUR LOCAL FISHING GROUNDS.

O'Donnells challenging each other's right to dominion over this meeting point of their territorial ambitions.

Commas was once the shooting preserve of Lord Erne, but was taken over and divided into banks for anyone who wanted turf and the rest was used as sheep grazing.

The last quarter of a mile of the road was suitable only for tractors and we walked our bicycles along the edges.

Their was a lot of camaraderie in Commas as all our neighbours had banks there...Priors, Byrnes, Darcys, McGoverns and Tommy Farrelly. "Is he poking for rats?" Tommy would say of anyone who didn't keep a straight edge bank. We had some very happy times in Commas, and Enda and myself would have contests jumping the bogholes which he invariably won and one time having failed to reach the far bank, my two feet became lodged in the side about six foot up from the ground and it was almost impossible to extricate myself.

We built our fire in the shelter of a clump of heather and boiled eggs and water for our tea and sometimes cooked rashers.

Commas had the best of black turf and one man would cut with the slean and in a practised motion throw the turf off the slean to the catcher on the bank, who filled up the wheelbarrow and brought them out to where they would dry. If your muscles weren't aching after the journey to get to the workplace, I'll guarantee they were by the end of the day.

We kept our tools and cooking implements hidden among the clumps of heather, although nobody would steal them, but they might hide them and have a sly laugh as you spent half a morning searching. We once tried to introduce "new technology" to the operation and took a day to drive "Neddy" the whole way to Commas, having decided that with his help we could dispense with the wheelbarrow by getting him to pull a sheet of galvanize on which we placed the newly cut turf out to the spot for spreading and later on he could carry the dry turf in creels or bordogs down the bank to the road where they would be loaded into a tractor trailer. We reckoned that we could cut down the labour and time significantly. Neddy could carry two creels and quickly and all we had to do was fill and empty them.

Both these ideas worked in theory, but the donkey was a

stallion and he would be missing every morning, having gone walkabout in search of female company. It would be hours before we could find him and get him back to the workface, and if we couldn't find him we had to take his place, although we only carried one creel at a time.

The spread turf would develop a dry skin after a day or two and then were turned to repeat the process on the other side. All being well and the weather holding they were then footed and finally clamped ready for despatch.

Commas was in reality part of the mountain and was above the treeline so you had no shelter when the rain started and had to run hell for leather and take shelter under the bridge at the end of the lane. This was fine and dandy, but if the shower was very heavy or prolonged, the water rose quickly and forced you from your refuge.

There were two other things you had to look out for. The midges, our own version of the mosquito, could arrive like lightning, especially in the evening and they were truly a ravenous horde. They would instantly attack, their effect being the airborne equivalent of thousands of miniature piranha as they tried to devour any piece of skin or scalp they landed on. There was no defence only the remedy of flight although one wag reckoned that two brothers who never washed were consequently never bothered by the midges as they were unable to penetrate the armour which many years aversion to soap and water had added to their skin.

The other problem was even more deadly. The mist or fog would descend without warning and you had to leave promptly when it appeared as you literally could not see more than a yard when it settled in, and we spent several hours crawling our way along the road the first time it appeared.

Commas was also a rich repository of stories from the characters who interspersed their work with a tale or two to liven up the day. Somedays there might be hundreds working in the bog and there was a great interplay between various "boyos". One of our "neighbours" in the turfbank sense was Andrew Big Hughie and he set up what looked like a water pump which he would go and duly pump for several minutes. Naturally enough this attracted the attention of others as we had to use the brackish bog water for tea and cooking and numerous individuals suddenly discovered pressing reasons for coming over in our direction only to discover that it was one cross piece of wood nailed to another to simulate a pump. After a few sly attempts at examination they skulked off without even mentioning it. Saving face is not restricted to the Orientals.

The same gentleman told us many lurid tales of London's Soho district and how somebody got parted from their money and didn't get what they had been promised into the bargain, and judging from the sting in the tales maybe the ones whose bargains were unfulfilled were the lucky ones.

The ride home in the evening was worth all the hard work. We flew down the mountain road, with the recklessness of youth, often passing cars whose drivers had more respect for the sharp bends and the steep hills.

When the years work in the bog was finished our group, with panjurs, saucepans, frying pans, sleans and wheelbarrows tied to the bikes, careered down those hills like the catering corps of a medieval chieftains' rag tag army hurrying to the plunder of some unsuspecting town.

The turf were soon drawn home to the safety of the barn. Nobody left them too long in the bog once they were dried. It would be offering too much temptation to anyone who maybe hadn't enough to last the winter. In fact there was a story of one man who noticed that small amounts were being regularly taken from his clamps and decided to put a stop to it. When he had brought most of his crop home he left a couple of dry clamps and inserted a shotgun cartridge into one of the turf he had left behind, gluing it together. The culprit and his wife got the shock of their lives one cold night when they put on a blazing fire!

Aunt Maggie built retaining walls at intervals in the barn to keep the rest of the turf from falling about as they were used up during the winter, and took pride in their management and stock control, with the blocks of wood and sticks all within easy reach.

# 4

## *Shades of Autumn.*

The weeks had flown by. The swallows who had built their nests in the barn were flying higher and higher, checking the currents and weather patterns for the marathon trip to southern Africa. Their new brood were flaunting their independence, showing off silky flying skills, and building their strength and body mass for the same trip which they would embark on a few weeks after their parents.

We too started preparing for the winter and a certain dry day was awaited to cut the oats. Dolly and his Deering machine provided the horse power once more, and one man sat in the seat driving and another with a triangle shape with a long handle depressed the collector to form sheafs. The rest of the workforce followed behind lifting and tying the sheafs and arranging them in stucks...that is six sheafs standing with another pulled down, wrong way up, over their heads to ward off any unwelcome rain, before they could be carried home on the cart and built in a reek awaiting the thresher.

This needed a "meitheall", and help came from all the neighbours. The "Pat Toms" arrived early with the thresher, and it was powered by belts run from the power drive of the tractor.

A hearty breakfast of bacon , eggs  and sausages with home baked bread and large steaming mugs of tea, so strong a mouse could walk on it, and we were ready.

One man was on top of the reek, lifting the sheaves, untying them, and passing them to his colleague who manoeuvred them down into the thresher where the machinery separated the ears from the straw. The straw was discharged from the machine in one location and taken away and stacked. The ears came out a chute into a hessian sack which was constantly attended by another neighbour and carried off to the shed , not forgetting that it had to be immediately replaced by an other sack to that none of the oats would spill on the ground.

The dogs, especially the terriers, would be on constant alert, and their quarries were any presumptuous rats who had dared to set up home and kitchen in the oat reek. Very few of these safely negotiated the distance from the reek to the nearest ditch. It normally took only half a day to finish the oats and then the whole 'caravan' after more tea, would set off to the next neighbour who had booked the thresher.

The hay which had been left in cocks in the meadows, was now brought in and built in pikes or reeks in the haggard. The hay was built on the cart to be brought in from the outlying meadows but the cocks from the nearby meadows were dragged in by chains attached to Dolly's collar. We always built pikes rather than reeks. These contained about ten cocks and were built on bases of sally bushes to keep any damp at bay. One man pitched the hay up to another who tramped it to make it even and stable. They were trimmed carefully and a thatch of rushes put on top and tied down with criss-crossing ropes.

The biggest 'meithell' of all was picking the potatoes. Before the mechanical digger made its appearance Father and Frank would dig the ridges out all day and when Enda and myself came home from school we spent many a long cold evening picking the potatoes and carrying them to the heaps. These were a cleared area, on a dry spot with a layer of rushes at the bottom and a further layer on each side of the triangle shaped mound in which we placed the crop. Then the whole lot was covered with a layer of mould about three inches thick to keep out the rain and frost. Our hands were bitterly cold as you had to rub the clay off the tubers and after a while you could not feel any sensation in your fingers while your back felt as if some malignant force had twisted you into a ball from which there was no release.

This cutting and picking continued for several weeks, depending on the weather as it was no use at all to pick and store wet potatoes in the heaps as they would all rot. Even when all the ridges had been dug, it was still not over and they might go quickly

COMNAS — A WINDSWEPT EXPANSE ABOVE THE TREE
LINE — AN EVER CHANGING KALEIDOSCOPE OF COLOURS.

over the whole area, turning the soil to capture the ones who had escaped us the first time around. Some of these might have spots of green colour where the sun had touched them and were stored separately for the pigs.

The arrival of the mechanical digger changed all that and it was one piece of modernisation which I wholeheartedly welcomed.

The workers were arranged in twos, and each pair had a metal bathpan, about half the size of an ordinary bath with handles on each end. The job required about twenty pickers and was the largest example of the co-operative spirit which the small farms, with very little organisation, produced at short notice.

The digger wound its way up one ridge or drill (we had now started sowing the seeds in drills to speed up the sowing and make the 'stievein' redundant), and down one on the far side. And the pickers ,bent double  and  carrying the bathpan between them patrolled their area, anxious to avoid the ignominy and jeers which would follow on if they held up the digger when it came round again. The long range scouts had already brought back word to the main army and the white knights, the seagulls, competed aggressively  for the potatoes and had the bonus of having the worms, slugs and snails all to themselves...a veritable hoard of delicacies.

You needed to keep a sharp eye about you not to miss any potatoes, and an even sharper one to avoid the guided missiles... any tubers found to be rotten, and used as ammunition by some latchyko who thought you weren't looking.

Harvesting the spuds was back breaking and at half way stage (or full time if there was any danger of rain) a massive feed of the crop itself, complimented by boiled bacon and cabbage was eagerly devoured and washed down with bottles of Guinness and cola or fizzy orange for the younger brigade.

As one farmer completed the picking and storing of the potatoes, the whole caravan again moved on to the next neighbour, the old back had to gird itself for a repeat performance - the second of many,  and without a break if the weather remained favourable. The larger proportion of the fodder and crops were now safely won and stored. Attention turned to the onions, turnips, carrots and the like but these were only sideshows to the main events and if everything had gone according to plan it was a satisfied and relieved farmer who watched the green leaves turn to gold.

# 5

## *Darker Nights.*

The wind coming down from the mountains or across the
lake hit the face with a sharper edge. The cattle became a little
tamer, even the drystock that we normally didn't have much
contact with came closer. The soft showers were no longer as soft,
sometimes they included drops of hail and now the top of the
Cuilcagh mountains often sported a hoary head of hair like a close
friend growing old and venerable with age.

The last remaining outdoor jobs took on an urgency. We
knew time was running out. We battened down our hatches. The
last of the hay was secured in the reeks and they were thatched,
trimmed and tied. A good dry, sunny day with a light wind was
availed of to winnow the oats. A sheet was spread on the ground
and the oats thrown up a couple of handfuls at a time to let the
wind blow the chaff away and five or six full bags were loaded on
Dolly's cart  and taken to Bellaness mill to be ground into meal -
porridge for the year.

Father would be there all day and we had the form, built
by Frank at the Technical School in Bawn, ready in its place
between the stairs and the fire, to store the bags of meal. It could
be a long, long day at the mill. This was their busy time and the
other farmers would all be clamouring to have their supply of oats
ground as well.  It might be very late, eleven or twelve o'clock  and
Mum would have sent Frank out several times to listen. The hope
was that he would hear Dolly's hooves as he clipped clopped home
along the Ardara lane. Frank must have been fed up with being
sent out to listen and in response to Mum's question "Well, did you
hear them coming?", he famously replied , "S'pose I did and S'pose
I didn't". Eventually Father arrived and we all crowded round and

helped any way we could as the bags were carried in and placed on the form. A good percentage of the next twelve months food supply was safe and sound.

The onions were picked and hung up by the stalks in the barn. Our erstwhile neighbours, the swallows had long departed on their migration and their nests of clay worked to a consistency of cement, and lined with moss, animal hair and wool stood like deserted temples of some long forgotten gods, awaiting the birds return in the spring as the family units always come back to their own freeholds.

The mornings were getting colder, there was a noticeable chill in the air and the farmers on the higher hills were getting the byres and sheds ready "to bring in the cattle". The cows would be first. Most of these would now be pregnant and due to calve the following spring. The longer you could keep them out in the fields the less fodder you would need and if your own supply was not enough to last the full winter it would be expensive to buy more. But the goodness was gone out of the grass and although there was still some there, "the feeding was not in it", and soon all the livestock would need supplements of the sweet smelling hay and a handful or two of oats for Dolly.

Winters' messengers, the first flurries of snow, concentrated everybody's mind. There was no longer any possibility of delaying the inevitable. The cattle were brought in and settled into their winter quarters and now they were tended like sick relatives, their food brought to them twice a day, plenty to drink and their stalls cleaned regularly. They provided the milk which paid for a lot of our food, and we sold their progeny to buy more. In return we catered to their every need and treated them like minor royalty. We didn't put toothpaste on their brushes but we certainly did soften their drinking water, that is put a small amount of hot water into their buckets of drinking water to take the chill out of it, as the weather got colder and frostier.

The drystock, who would be wintered out in the open, some in outlying land maybe a half a mile or more away, the legacy of innumerable divisions of farms among sons and the acquisition of fields through marriage dowries over hundreds of years, had to be supplied with hay. We carried this in bundles , tied with ropes, on our backs over intervening farms, over ditches and drains, thorn quicks and wire fences through hail rain and snow, and when you reached your destination the animals would almost trample you in their desperation to get at the fodder.

Many of the cows would still be milking and we milked them morning and evening sitting on three legged stools with a bucket held between our knees so that a sudden kick from the cow would not spill it. To us it was liquid gold.

The muscles in our lower arms were highly developed from milking and we were young, fit and strong but even still milking nine or ten cows, if you had to do it on your own, left an ache or two in its wake.

The trees were now bare. The golden mantle of Autumn was gone and only the holly and the ivy kept their good looks. It was no wonder that both were of special significance, the red berried holly was our Christmas decoration and the mysterious ivy the material sans pareil of the magicians and the Celtic priests - the druids.

The area took on a surreal aspect. The cold mists and fog were tied to the bleak trees by countless spiders webs and when frost and ice claimed their own places the effect was multiplied a hundred fold and the lanes and byways became the hallways and corridors of a magical kingdom cocooned and protected in our impenetrable redoubt by our mountains, lakes, rivers and marshes that had proved to be a no go area for invaders for thousands of years.

# 6

## *Corratillan School.*

Settled on the left side of the road, a little bit more than halfway as one journeyed from Swanlinbar to Ballinamore, the school rested, cut into the pale grey hill.

Folding doors, divided the building into two classrooms, one for the juniors and the other for the seniors. Outside a wall from the back of the school to the top of the yard created a further division between the playtime areas of the boys and girls. With two cloakrooms and two dry toilets, one on each side of the afore mentioned wall, Corratillan provided all the facilities for the educational requirements of lower Corlough.

It catered for between fifty and sixty pupils, and had two teachers...usually a lady for the juniors and a man for the seniors.

At the tender age of four, in my knitted suit, I was entrusted to the untender mercies of my brother and sister, and started the trek along sandy roads to my fate with destiny. We were accompanied down the first part of the journey by the Byrnes, Smiths and McGoverns, and received reinforcements at various points along the way; the Gregorys at the "cross of the Spring", the Darcys, Rita Rourke and the Reillys at Jim Micks Hill, the Priors at the nearway leading from their house up past Pat Priors and at Phil Thomas's cross by a veritable host - nearly all called McGovern - and the Dolans...until forming roughly one half of the schools population our motley crew arrived at Corratillan.

Now was the parting of the ways and arrested by the hand of the lady teacher I was deposited in the row of seats near the fire. The only contribution my immediate group , the infants, made was to play with Marla, draw pictures of cats and dogs or any farm animal by pencil on our jotter, and kick each other under the desks. All my animals looked exactly the same and resembled no animal under the sun.

The playtime breaks were a new experience entirely. For the first day or indeed for the first week my brother and sister kept a benign eye on my welfare but gradually withdrew to their own friends and games and in the interests of survival, I had to gird my loins and apply a well aimed kick with my nailed boot - small though it was, it was still quite deadly to the shin of one member of the McGovern clan.

He would probably have gladly throttled me there and then but such was his loss of face through hopping around in pain that I had the indian sign on him from then on.

We spent four years in the junior room before promotion to the senior side of the school, only ever returning to the junior side for music, which in my case never materialised as I was excused music lessons, or perhaps the better wording should be banished from them on the grounds that I was tone deaf and couldnt sing a note . This was not before I received four strokes of the cane for my efforts in rendering "Three Blind Mice", the teacher being convinced that I was being deliberately dreadful, whereas in truth I was delivering the refrain in my best dulcet tones. The episode was unluckier still for Thomas Jude Logan, who was standing next to me and received even more strokes for laughing at my effort.

In the 'seniors', life got perceptively tougher. The cane was much more in evidence - a long bamboo thing with a a caimin or handle on it. We developed our own method of dealing with this and pushing it up the chimney and resting it on the ventilation ledge when the master wasn't looking was very effective at least until the said master, on brushing the fireplace prior to lighting the fire was suddenly the recipient of a half a dozen canes from further up the opening. Our own intrepid trio was to the fore in the never ending battle against the cane. Cyril Prior, Paddy Smith and yours truly developed our own method of making the canes disappear now that the chimney hideout was no longer operative, and in this operation we were unwittingly aided by the Lenten devotions.

Before leaving school on a Friday evening we would leave a window very slightly open. We then went home as normal, ate our dinner, did our jobs around the place and then as piously as ever went to the evening devotions in Corlough, but when these ended we put our plan into action. We cycled home the back way down through Cortoon and hid our bikes. It was now easy to enter our schoolroom through the open window and lay our hands on the hated cane.

So far so good but when has any good plan ended while things are going well?

Paddy Smith couldn't resist getting out Miss Byrne's melodion and attempting to prove his musical abilities and we had to make a very quick getaway as the music or rather the noise attracted the attention of Paddy Martin whose house was in the meadow across from the school.

Even when we got rid of the officially manufactured cane it was still not the end of the matter. The master, as the male teacher was called, introduced a fiendish ploy of his own to replenish his stock. He would send one of us out to cut a sally rod from the quick or hedge near the school, knowing it was going to be used on one of our friends and maybe even on oneself. We hit back against this by cutting it thinly near the middle with a razor blade with the result that it would not last long and might even break after its first use. And if none of the aforementioned remedies were available to us we fell back on an old bit of witchcraft - namely to have a horse's hair across your hand as we were being caned, having been assured on the authority of a past pupil who was obviously taking the mickey, that it would break the cane...but I am sorry to say our knowledge of the arcane arts was not up to the task.

One of the male teachers during our time was a master Sharkey who had a penchant for applying snuff to his nostrils and then spend some time combing his remaining two lonely tufts of hair on his temples while using the bottom of his snuff box as a mirror. Master Sharkey was quite generous in his use of the cane, only requiring a reasonable provocation and one day it arrived with a vengeance.

The master was sitting at his desk - his sandwiches spread in front of him, and pouring a cup of tea from his flask whilst at the same time Michael Oliver Fox was lining up a freekick in the

CORRATELLAN SCHOOL.

football game being played outside in the boys playground. As fate would ordain the two events came together in that Michael's kick was not on target and instead the ball sped straight like an arrow from hell through the window spreading glass splinters all round and removing the master's sandwiches, cup of tea, flask and snuff box from the desk, scattering them over the floor like leaves in Autumn ! The cane administrated punishment to all, bystanders as well as players, without discrimination.

Sharkey's reign ended a few years later when he was found attempting to swim in the river below Feehans although there was only about six inches of water in it at the time. It seems that the power of snuff was no defence against being driven round the bend by his charges...our goodselves.

There was a teacher named Boyle who presided a few years before my time who had a down on Aidan Jim Mick. It was known by everyone that on the day of his departure, being driven in a horse and trap he had to keep hopping from side to side to avoid blows being aimed at him with a spade wielded by a brother of Aidan's.

I can only remember two lady teachers - one Miss Maureen Byrne who later went to live in Dublin, and Mrs Reilly who lived a half a mile away towards Ballinamore, and had two very goodlooking daughters Lily and Kathleen who also attended the school. There were several classes in each room and whichever one was being taught assembled round Mrs. Reilly's large desk. Her chain had an oval type depression and I remember Cyril, before she would sit down, would place a ruler across the depression and it would sway up and down slightly when she sat on it but obviously her corsets must have been of sufficient strength to nullify any feeling.

Football was one of our chief entertainments during the lunch break but our version did not conform fully with the rules of the Gaelic Athletic Association or indeed any association, we respected no authority or rules but our format probably resembled the original version of the game established in the latter half of the nineteenth century.

We divided the total roll call into two halves, threw the rubber or more likely rag ball, depending on the finances available, into the middle. and did our best to force it by kicks, punches, shoulder charges or anything else you could think of through the other side's goal - two stones or jackets placed eight feet apart.

This game, I soon learned, was a marvellous opportunity for settling old scores or starting whole new enmities, and it didn't really matter if your enemy was on your team or not, the smug satisfaction was still as sweet as nectar.

Football did not occupy all our playdays. We had other games, for instance "JAIL" or "TIG".

In playing "Jail" we selected about six of the bigger boys and their job was to chase, capture and imprison the others in an area, surrounded by two walls near the entrance. Three or four warders guarded those who had been captured while the others, like bounty hunters, chased the free ones all over the school yard and hauled them off to the clink. It certainly wasn't easy to get them all as there were paths on the top of the ditches, between blackthorn bushes, where the fugitives could make a stand and by any means try to prevent the jailers from getting hold of them. Some would even jump the ditches and hedges into Reilly's land and range far and wide like the rapparies of old to maintain their freedom.

"Tig" was less elaborate and was played by appointing one person who in order to transfer the responsibility had to chase and touch another in order to make that person the pursuer instead. Our playground, being limited in size, did not give us full scope for this endeavour so we blithely ignored all borders and fences and jumped ditches and drains whether as the hunter or hunted. Many a day, despite official disapproval, we ran wildly over the farmers fields, only returning when the teacher, complete with swinging cane, could be seen contemplating the pros and cons of jumping the three strands of barbed wire which had acted as no deterrent to us. Mostly the teachers and the local farmers had a very good attitude to all this. They ignored it, rightly believing that young people will be young people and that no great harm was being done.

Stone throwing , believe it or not, was a great favourite of ours. Some playtimes, we would just laze about, with a ready supply of stones at hand, waiting for the seagulls, who came circling and whooping, looking for crumbs of our home baked bread. When we judged they were within reach, at a given signal, we would let forth a volley worthy of the stone throwers of ancient Persia. I am delighted to state that our aims against the seagulls were about as useful as a blind man with a sniper's rifle, so the seagulls were in no danger and to judge from their flights, were well aware of this. In fact it sometimes looked as if they timed their graceful swoops to get us into trouble as they made a great show of gliding by the windows.

One particular stone throwing day, as our tenth volley landed in Martins meadow, Paddy Martin came over from his house and told us to stop, but Paddy Smith, playing to the gallery, jumped out on the road, and declared that he would do it again whereupon he wished, whereupon Paddy Martin lifted him and threw him over the ditch into the meadow!

Corratillan school was the setting for our first experience of the film makers art - a health and hygiene film in cartoon form, probably produced under the aegis of Dr. Noel Browne, the Minister for Health, extolling the virtues of looking after your teeth. It featured a baddie, a germ, looking remarkably like Bugs Bunny, who was dashing around rows of teeth showing the damage he could cause, when assisted by an excess of sweets and sugar. The moral was of course how you could put an end to his blackguarding by washing your teeth regularly and to start the whole process rolling we were each given a toothbrush and a small round box, smaller than a polish box of "Gibbs Peroxide toothpaste".

This gentle introduction to the care of our molars was followed in no short time by my first encounter with the ogre of my life...the dentist. He arrived a fortnight later complete with assistant and a fiendish collection of torture instruments worthy of De Sade himself.

He appropriated a teacher's desk, and a large part of one room and we were summoned class by class to await our turn for the inspection. This was not an assessment day only, oh no! When treatment was found to be necessary it was carried out there and then and in my case it required the extraction of half of one of my

THE WORKHOUSE BAWNBOY. DATING FROM THE TIME
OF THE FAMINE - NOW OVERGROWN WITH IVY.

front teeth, which had been broken for some years. Can you imagine having a tooth pulled out in a classroom in those days with very little in the way of pain deadening and at the end of the treatment walking the two miles home with a lump of cotton wool stuck in your mouth to stem the flow of blood resulting from the pulling of the roots, with, what seemed to me, the strength a man would exert in a tug of war contest. The event has remained etched in my consciousness for ever.

Our heating was by means of an open turf burning fire in each room and we were often sent out to gather sticks or "breshna" to get the turf lighted. There were plentiful supplies of turf in Corlough and each family sent in a supply, usually in a cart drawn by a donkey but if we needed a few urgently we often carried a few turf in with us in the morning from home.

Our desks were two seater affairs of wood and metal, with two hinged lid compartments for books, pens and pencils and an inkwell in the middle. The ink did not come in small labelled bottles...we made our own.

Blue powder was taken from the box in the cupboard and mixed in an enamel basin with clear water from the spring near the river. The proportion of each ingredient I no longer remember, but we made a hell of a lot of ink, stored it in earthenware jugs from which our inkwells were replenished at regular intervals. The ink making extravaganza invariable sparked off an ink war from the hidden supplies secreted from the production line and earned us a good hiding from our furious parents.

In the Summer we wore no shoes and no matter what the weather boffins say I can assure you that the weather in that season was both warmer and drier than now. Because of this we went home the nearway, past Paddy Priors and over the river on the stepping stones. Here, we stopped and fished for liebins. These were very small fish, and we caught these with worms on a rush which as soon as the liebin grabbed it we yanked them out on the bank. However the real advantage in going the nearway were the beautiful apples in Priors orchard, and we often helped ourselves liberally. But there were also juicy delicacies along the normal route home, namely the plums in Feehans garden.

The great day for plums was a Wednesday, as the shop

then closed for a half day and the family usually went up to Lahernahone near Ballyconnell, to visit Joe's brother Dessie, and we were able to sample the plums without fear of interruption...or so we thought.

One Wednesday, bold as brass ,we were high in the trees when old Pat walked in through the gate! In the stampede to get away, under the wire I tore as neat a "Z" into the back of my new corduroy jacket as the mark of ZORRO.

One of the great problems of going barefoot was acquiring stone bruises on your toes and later on when the main road was tarred it stuck to your feet in warm weather.

Moral retribution for taking the plums eventually caught up with me and it commenced when jumping down from the wall to the road. One Autumn I found it increasingly difficult to walk and the pain became unbearable if I kicked a football. It got so bad that I was unable to go to school so something had to be done about it. Doctors were not often called to our neck of the woods. They had to be paid - and there was also a belief that they were not much good. "He lost my brother during the big snow of '47. He wasn't able to do anything about the pneumonia!", my Mother often said and Doctor McLoughlin was never quite looked on in the same light again. So he was not called to view my unusable foot, nor was I brought to him, even though that would have reduced the cost...dispensing with the cost of his petrol I suppose.

One balmy Sunday evening, about eight months after the appearance of the first symptoms my Father put me on the bar of the bike and we set off up to the Blackrocks to see the local bonesetter..."The Rackard".

This "physician" had a thriving local practice putting back shoulders and other joints which had somehow escaped their ordained setting and it did not matter whether the patient was a bullock or a human...the treatment was the same and so was the charge! And it must be said he was quite successful, his chief attributes being a little knowledge, a lot of strength and no formality!

He enjoyed a few bottles of Guinness with my father while I sat there contemplating my fate, and he then examined my foot. Without elaborating on the problem or sharing his diagnosis he

THE FORMER DRUMLOUGHER SCHOOL. SEVERAL SCHOOLS
OF THIS DESIGN WERE BUILT AROUND THE EARLY
1950's INCLUDING MUNLOUGH.

pressed one of the old large pennies which was adorned with the hen and chickens with such pressure that the pain practically took my breath away. That was the treatment and after my Father had semi-surrepticiously placed the fee into the "Rackard's " pocket we left, and free-wheeled down the mountain on the Raleigh bicycle. Although the pain was quite awful you could not bleat on about it or cry as to do so would be a cardinal error for a boy in our society. The foot did not get much better and I was home from school for a long period and often stayed up with Aunt Maggie in her house.

One day walking near the apple trees in a pair of sandals with no socks, I noticed a small black spot like a speck of dust on the top of my foot. I scratched it away with my nail and a thorn, about one and a half inches long came out with it. This had obviously worked its way up through my foot and had entered when I jumped off the wall during one of our expeditions for plums.

No wonder the pain was so intense when the "Rackard" pressed the penny down on top of it...

# 7

## *Hours Together.*

The first lamp I remember was the twin wick oil lamp with a glass globe.

One evening my Father arrived home with a Tilley lamp. He had sold some calves in the fair in Ballinamore and decided to invest in a new lighting system.

This was a very different kettle of fish from the oil lamp. It came in several parts and was at the cutting edge of technology of its day. It boasted a body with a built-in pumping system, a round globe, a long hollow needle, a lighter, a gauze type mantle and a spare. You also needed oil to fuel it and a supply of methylated spirits.

The "Tilley" was looked at, and speculated upon from all angles and finally Father started the process.

To set it up and light it for the first time was not a simple operation. First of all the lamp was filled with oil. Next you assembled the needle vertically in its place inside the hollow tube which ran from the top of the oil container up through where the mantle would hang, and fixed the gauze mantle into position, making sure it was correct because you didn't get a second chance. Now methylated spirits was poured on the lighter and it was clipped around the hollow tube, a couple of inches below the mantle and lit with a match. This now burned the mantle into a round shape, as delicate as ash. The lamp was then pumped to increase the pressure inside and the "ON" switch was turned to allow the oil or paraffin to travel up the needle and emerge as a fine spray inside the mantle where it ignited, and and hey presto we had light.

We were flabbergasted at the new brightness. Corners that

we had barely seen at night before were now as bright as day and I found a sixpence that had eluded all dogged search parties up till then. But the great thing was that you could actually read without having the lamp against your ear. It was not rested on the table but instead replaced its predecessor the twin wick lamp hanging from the "S" hoop in the beam over the table, that being a precaution to insure, as Father put it, that nobody's big head would bump into it. Soon the downside became all too clear, there was no excuse for not doing homework. Now you could actually see the books.

The Tilley lamp was soon followed by two more luxuries-a cuckoo clock and a radio.

The Cuckoo clock arrived first. It was much the same as any of its genre of today or I suppose of the last hundred years or so, but it was new to us and created a bit of a stir in Teeboy. Neighbours called just before noon to see it Cuckooing. There we would stand, just before twelve o'clock, all waiting for the cuckoo to emerge. It was no use coming at 1pm because it would only cuckoo once but at twelve you really got value for your money.

The radio was a different matter altogether!

Ours was called a "BUSH " and boasted a wet battery - a see-through jar with two battery terminals and full of acid, and a built in handle for carrying it. It also had a large 'dry battery', which was fitted inside. The wet battery was affixed to leads at the side. It had an aerial to pick up the broadcasts and had to be fixed up as high as you could get it.

This piece of equipment was delivered by van from Martins in Ballinamore, set up and turned to Radio Eireann or Athlone as it was depicted on the dial. It was turned on religiously for the 'News' and just as religiously turned off afterwards.

All programmes were strictly censored by Mama and I vividly remember one of Sean O'Casey's plays "Murder at the Red Barn" getting short shrift when mother's attentive ear became aware that part of the subject matter was the consequence of sex outside marriage.

Broadcasts of Gaelic football and hurling matches were ok and so were political discussions even though opinions opposed to ours were not listened to without comment...the author, though out of range of the hearing of us youngsters, being told what was thought of him.

In the field of light entertainment, "Take the floor" with its host "Dinjo" was out in front by a mile and some of the neighbours would arrive in good time for its eight o'clock start. Dinjo was the equivalent of Bruce Forsyth on radio, cracking jokes - no dirty ones mind you...a few cheery songs, a couple of guest singers or comedians and he always did a commentary on a dance, a reel or jig which we assumed rightly or wrongly was being performed in the studio and with his "round the house and mind the dresser" and "Skim the floor" encouragements went on for several minutes. Whether the dance was genuine or faked we didn't know but he described it with more gusto than an American football commentator.

Everyone laughed loudly, drank their tea, and declared that he was the best crack they had ever heard.

With the passage of time competitors made their appearance. "Living with Lynch" and "Hal Roach", but we remained true to our first love.

A big fire of turf was always blazing to keep our visitors warm during the radio "Cabaret" show. But the fire was in its own right a potent sign of status and respectability as a house with a poor fire was just not quite the same. It probably had something to do with the Celtic reverence for fire - a remaining vestige of our sun worshipping ancestors or again as one irreverent wag once said, it was simply that without a good fire you would bloody well freeze to death!

A good fire might earn you kudos but we weren't silly enough to let it burn without a material gain, so during the show two ovens hung on the crook, bringing to life within their warm wombs two beautiful soda cakes with a cross cut into the top of each. It made a very satisfying spectacle, with the red hot coals of turf perched on the lids of each oven to ensure even baking top and bottom.

'Apres Dinjo', the well eared cards would be shuffled and dealt for "Twenty Five" at a penny a game. There followed much pounding of the table as trump cards came down, tricks were made and games won or saved. I have played many card games in different situations and company but "Twenty Five " can only be played by the Irish and by its very nature required an inquest or wake after each game, but may God help you if you beat the man with a low score and allow the top man to win out.

Card playing, or more properly "Twenty Five " playing was not confined to a few hours after "Dinjo", no. It was taken a lot more seriously than that and certain houses and nights were reserved for its exclusive enjoyment.

James and Joe Priors was definitely the top venue for the mens' games. Neither of the brothers had ever married and thus no attention seeking wives disrupted enjoyment of their all consuming passion. They milked their cows early on a Friday night and laid in some bottled Guinness and a bottle of Poteen. It was a scene from which we youngsters were barred until we had honed our skills and copied the mannerisms and arcane language of the game. There was always the risk of instant shame or total banishment if you made the wrong move too often.

Bank holidays or the close approach of Christmas provided great excuses for a grander setting and half barrels of Porter would be put on the fare with a special prize of a pig or with apologies to the parable, 'a fatted calf'.

We, the younger apprentices, to this time honoured ritual developed our own routine and between Priors, Byrnes, Smiths and our own house we had a weekly rota system for our age group. On many a quiet and starlit night we would walk the narrow lanes and cross the fields to the appointed house. It was an exclusive male experience, a priesthood without females, a golden age of pre-responsibility before the exciting and terrifying rules of the game would be changed and girls would enter the equation as unequal - yes unequal, but definitely more powerful players----the glamorous and sensual Queens of chess to our grey and fumbling pawns.

Before we graduated to cards we played other games - Ludo, Snakes and Ladders and Draughts, and often the these games, especially the Draughts could take on marathon proportions and last for hours.

Rings, a game with a board similar to a dartboard and rubber rings instead of darts was very popular as were marksmanship contests with small guns which fired rubber covered darts.

Every house we played in dispensed tea and cakes or currant bread, baked in the oven, and these memories have remained bright and warming over the years.

When the visitors who had come to make their 'ceilidh' were not playing cards or listening to the radio they told stories and we listened eagerly , especially to any irreverent ones which we could repeat to our friends at school in the coming days. Religion and Priests were often the subject matter as for example;

A new priest to the parish was doing his rounds, visiting his flock. He called in to the local forge to have a chinwag with the blacksmith who he thought might also be a storehouse of information.

"I've heard all about you (the priest had only been transferred from the neighbouring parish) that your sermons go on a bit and you know the men of this area like their sport on a Sunday."

The Priest drew himself up to his full majesty and proclaimed loftily "I have to preach the word of God." "If I were you" replied the blacksmith," I'd just say mass and let them all go to hell."

Priests and the length of time they took to conduct the services came in for a good bit of mocking and irreverence as the alleged conversation between two parishioners about their new Padre illustrates;

"Be jeepers he takes an awful long time",

"Ah I don't know...what you lose on the Our Father you gain on the Hail Mary".

Funerals came in for a bit of fun poking as well even though you might expect them to be solemn affairs. A well known local undertaker called 'A' was taken to task by the deceased's wife about the quality of the Habit or Shroud with which he had encased her beloved as he lay in his coffin. 'A' drew himself up to his full height and silenced her with these words "My dear , good attire was never a habit of his"!

To dig a grave in Corlough was a herculean task. The ground was full of large rocks or boulders and they sat in heavy clay which had to be dug out by pick, spade and shovel. Once the grave had been dug it was essential to have the internment completed as soon as possible as the sides and ends were very likely to fall in and necessitate more digging, and the whole thing would be ten times worse if it was raining which was more often the case than not.

A Man from outside the parish was being buried in Corlough and the funeral was being conducted by a young dedicated priest from his adopted parish. The cortege was slowly winding its way up the hill and past the wall. The newly dug grave was inside the wall and the foreman of the diggers were getting very alarmed as bits of the grave's walls were starting to crumble in and they believed that it would be unusable if the procession continued at its present rate round by the main entrance. He couldn't wait any longer and, popping his head over the wall, said "Father if I were you I'd handball him in here while there's still room for him."

The other main religion, the Church of Ireland did not escape either. There was one told about a wealthy Church of Ireland man named Croker who was approaching the end of his days. His family had sent for the local vicar and he was trying to ease the old man's mind. "T'is a far far better place to which you are going" he intoned. Mr. Croker lifted himself up on his elbows in the bed, looked out the window at his rolling acres and his fine Friesian cattle for a minute, "I doubt it" he said, and dropped back dead. "I doubt it said Croker" was the standard retort when someone disbelieved a tale from then on.

All humour is at somebody's expense and ours was no different. They told the story about Old Jimmy, whose culinary taste was not very extensive. He was given a lift up to Dublin by a group going to see the All Ireland Football Final. I don't think he even went in to the match but walked around the city as it was his first and only visit. They would tease out what happened to him "What did you have for dinner?" And innocent Old Jimmy who had incurred the wrath of a white gloved Garda on Traffic Duty in O'Connell street by standing in front of him and exclaiming "I'll tell you something my bucko, you'll sleep tonight", would innocently reply "Mashed potato and green roundy balls."

Cameras were a new fangled arrival in the area and it

wasn't long before we heard of a local farmer who had instructed a photographer at the Farmers Ball to "Take the half of me and the whole of Mary".

Although the ceilidhs are not as common as before the humour has in no way been diminished but has largely been concentrated in the smaller pubs, especially those without any loud bellowing music. I recently heard a few in a pub in Carrigallen. One of them concerned a Scotsman called Robbie who lived about five miles from the town for many years. Most nights he would walk in to Carrigallen for a few drinks. Well one cold blustery night he was winding his way home and decided to have a cigarette. The windy conditions made lighting up difficult and he turned his shoulder against the wind to stop the match going out. He eventually succeeded in lighting his cigarette and resumed walking only to find after another hour and a half that he was back in Carrigallen.

That same night that I heard about Robbie there was a poor old devil I'll call John, who was obviously not the brightest spark around, and his 'friends' were drawing him out about current affairs. Mr. Bin Laden was on every newscast at that time and some teaser would address a question to him "Would Bin Laden be any relation to the Ladens of Arigna?" "I suppose he must...there both in construction" John replied. "No that not Bin Laden" rejoined the teaser "That's skip Laden."

# 8

## *Our Own Day.*

We were certain believers in the Lords command not to work on the seventh day but we didn't take his advice on resting. Determined to enjoy it to the full we laid our plans after meeting at Mass, as there were no phones in general use in those days...only one in the Post Office and that would only be used to call a doctor or more likely a vet in a dire emergency.

Gaelic Football was our passion. We tried Hurling once and cycled down to Swanlinbar to get some hurleys but our lack of skill left most of our group with badly bruised shins, black eyes, bleeding noses and quite a few cuts on the old noggins...so we went back to our first love.

This was when the 'Wran' money collected on St. Stephens day came in handy and a couple of lads were sent off to buy a good football that would last for the year.

Footballs then contained an inner tube with valve, laced inside a leather cover and when it got wet would hit you with the force of a cannon ball and our area was blessed with more rain than we desired. The weight of the ball could easily turn your thumb backwards and if it hit you in the face or sometimes even in a worse place you could be a spectator for the rest of the match.

We weren't all kitted out in full regalia by any means...very few had a complete kit and most were attired in a shirt, a pair of old trousers cut down into shorts and if you were lucky a pair of football boots, but many a player took the field in his hob nailed boots or wellingtons, and one or two played barefoot - although you had to be of a very hardy nature to do this.

Matches with neighbouring parishes always took on a keener edge and many ended up with a good old "fracas" involving players and spectators alike. At some venues it could get a bit hairy when you went near the sidelines as a disgruntled fan of your opponents could take a swipe at you when you were off guard. There was one middle aged lady, complete with stick, who prowled the sideline, and if you had tackled her son you were inviting severe and painful retribution from the said implement.

Our football field had a bit of a hill in the middle so from the far goals you would not be able to see the whole field. But God help you if you were the goalkeeper and allowed your attention to wander as suddenly half a dozen hairy fellows could come flying over the hill and the ball would be past you for a goal before you could regain your position.

Age was not a subject for too much attention, even when putting out under fourteen or under sixteen teams and I can assure you that several of the stars of those teams were already shaving for several years.

Away games, especially if far up the county, were a bit like an expedition and all types of motor vehicles were commandeered for the journey. And if lady luck did not smile on our efforts on that day, our trainer P. Francis, a man who gave many many years of dedicated service to football in the parish, could often be heard telling the opponents "Wait till we get you down to our field", well knowing that knowledge of its peculiar nature would certainly even things up in the return match.

Some of the matches, the friendlies, which did not count in championships or leagues, provided the best fun of all. There was one player who had no knowledge of football or its rules but compensated in unbounded enthusiasm. He often played barefoot and seemed to be immune to pain as he often played on with bits of toenails and flesh hanging off from impact with some players boots - and don't forget the studs were made of steel then. Players on his own team would egg him on and I remember on one occasion he was advised before the start to make sure that a certain footballer on the other side, who was very talented, did not get any scores. When the first high ball came into the area our stalwart levelled his opponent who had just made a fantastic high catch. A free kick was granted and the fouled player said nothing but a minute or so later the same thing happened again. This time the downed man did object and vehemently, but our man, who was without a trace of guile in the world, calmly replied "Dammy I was put on here to do a job on you and there's no need to take it it like that ".

The man who had just been levelled for the second time simply burst into laughter as he now knew that some of the Smart Alecs had set the whole thing up and he had a good idea of the culprits as all knew each other well.

Despite any injuries or fights nobody remained enemies for long and whenever they met even many years afterwards and maybe thousands of miles away the bond of friendship and camaraderie was always strong.

Not every Sunday was spent playing football in large groups. Nine or ten of us often played in P. Priors field and when we finished the game we journeyed down to the lake, to the "black banks" to do some fishing. Our fishing rods were hazel, cut from the plentiful supplies dotting the glens, and we affixed a line and hook, with a cork for a float and worms for bait.

Our quarry were perch and roach and we usually caught a few and often fished on until the moon was high over Hunts grove. Getting to and from the "black banks" so called because the water was darker there as the area on that side of the lake was boggy, was an exercise in survival. The bog adjoining the lake had been cut for turf over the millenia and now resembled a death trap of pathways and bottomless pits covered by lichen and bog cotton grasses which we called "shaking scraw". If you were on your own and fell into one of these you would never get out. Our parents must have had great faith in our instinct for life as we were allowed to negotiate this area with only an occasional warning "to be careful" and at night at that.

When we ran out of luck at the black banks there was nothing for it but get on our bikes and go off to the Blackwater river at Glencourthna. Now you could be virtually assured of catching fish here. Granted they were small but we often carried home twenty or thirty of them on a forked piece of Willow tied to the handlebar.

We never seemed to be able to catch the larger fish especially roach which we could see transversing the shallower stretches of the Blackwater. We finally hit on a plan and sewed several large hessian sacks together and on a certain Sunday arrived with our newly constructed net , determined to go after the big ones. But we were not greedy, at least not too greedy and decided that we would only keep a certain number and release the others so as not to reduce the stocks.

We did manage to corral a shoal towards one shallow stretch and with the hessian net spread wide we were cock a hoop. The Roach did not share our elation and turning round with a few effortless flicks of their tails they eluded our net and disappeared. We were so disappointed at the failure of our plan that we didn't bother anymore that day but instead threw stones at the corks of anybody fishing on the other side of the river. Enda was very good at fishing, and caught the biggest perch I have ever seen at the black banks.

Trout fishing was a different skill. We never perfected the art of fly fishing but were quite adept at catching trout in the traditional manner when there was a brown flood in the river after heavy rain, with worms again being the bait.

Frank had his own way of fishing for trout and his method of liming was highly successful if completely illegal. He also had a method of catching pike by means of a poor old frog attached to a set hook and being left in the lake overnight with the strong line tied to a tree. He did manage to catch a monstrous pike one day which I was given the job of cleaning out, cutting into portions and boiling in a large pot. It was delicious.

# 9

## *The Family Unit.*

My father was born in the townland of Ardlougher, in the parish of Kildallon, near Ballyconnell and at the age of ten was sent down to Teeboy, Corlough to live with his uncle Peter.

This was quite common in those days and the idea was that the youngster would be a help and company around the place and inherit the farm, there being no other immediate heirs.

His duties included helping with the mowing of the meadows and corn with a scythe and on hearing of this his father James came down from Ardlougher with a pair of horses and mowing machine which was the first such machine to be seen in Teeboy.

In his teens he joined the Republican volunteers in the War of Independence and was 'on the run' from his new home for almost four years. It didn't mean that he was away continually but had to be prepared to move quickly to safe houses or out into the hills at a moments notice to avoid capture or death by raiding parties of British soldiers, Auxiliaries or Black and Tans.

Aunt Maggie often told me how he and a colleague, one of the Byrnes lay in a cornfield while British soldiers searched the area around the edges.

He took part in the attack on the combined military/police post in Swanlinbar and later took the anti-treaty side at the time of the split. He never talked much about the struggle but did once tell me of a funny incident, somewhat related, which occurred during that time.

It was naturally impossible to buy ammunition or gunpowder during that war and he was one of those who learned how to make it. The Thady McGoverns, a family who lived a few hundred yards up the road would often ask him to make some powder for their own personal use in hunting and he arranged to call up on a certain evening to make some. He told them the ingredients that would be required and that it would have to be heated in a frying pan.

On his arrival on the appointed evening they had all the raw materials to hand but instead of a low heat coming from the ashes at the end of the fire they had a semi inferno blazing in the fireplace. My father had a devilish sense of humour and instead of pointing out the error of their ways he allowed one of them to put the pan, complete with its lethal mixture, over the burning fire, while making sure that he himself was near the door. The resultant bang removed most of the holders clothes and his eyebrows to boot and scattered the pots, pans and the kettle all over the kitchen!

During the "Troubles" the people stopped bringing their complaints or cases to the official police - the Royal Irish Constabulary, and instead brought them to the Republican movement who thus took over law and order responsibility on a local level, and gradually set up their own police and court system. The penalty for a sheep stealer might be for instance to spend a day or two working on the farm of the aggrieved party, or maybe taken to an island in a lake and left there for a day or two to cool their heels, as a kind of solitary confinement which had the beautiful advantage that it didn't cost anything.

My mother's name was Bridget Smith and she lived in upper Teeboy. Her father had visited America. He was a tall strong man...very forbidding, and as youngsters we had a great fear of him. He used to shave in the garden in front of the house, with a basin of water on the window sill and a mirror propped between the basin and the glass of the window. His razor was a long cut-throat which he sharpened on a rubber strap, and may God help you if you made a noise and caused him to nick himself with the cut-throat.

Grandad and Aunt Maggie lived in a mudwalled, three room house, with a long lane leading from the back up to the upper road. There front garden was arranged like a courtyard with a stone wall and gap to the meadow which had rows of daffodils along the top. Beautiful red and white rose trees clung to the walls around the windows along the left and a massive apple tree stood guard. The sheds and byre were on the right and there was a very large fruit garden also on the right with a lot of apple trees, black and red currants, gooseberry bushes, and a raised area for the hay rick.

My mother and Aunt Maggie had a brother and two sisters in America and another brother died during the big snow storm in Nineteen forty seven.

Grandad was getting quite old by then and Aunt Maggie didn't like them living alone so one or two of us had to stay with them on a continuous basis. On many a lonely night when Enda and myself were staying with them for the night 'minding them', Aunt Maggie would walk out into the front garden in the middle of the night , and imagine she was talking to her brother Patrick who had died in the big snow. She was convinced that the lights we could see in the distance were "lost souls on the moor tonight" rather than the "will-o-the wisp". She had missed out on going to America with her brother Phil as she stood on a broken bottle and lost a lot of blood which seemed to have had a lasting detrimental effect on her. She missed Phil enormously after he went to America as he was a happy go-lucky extrovert who joined the New York police and never came home again. It was with good reason that the farewell party before emigrants set off was known as the "American wake".

She remembered his exploits when young like carrying a sheet of ice from a pond and laying it in front of James Priors house who promptly skidded and fell on his backside on the ice on rushing out to investigate the loud knocking on his door.

My mother Bridget was the youngest of the family and was privileged in those days to have received a secondary education and teacher training at a convent school in Carrick on Shannon. She reminisced now and then about the time spent there and recalled when the local bishop and associated dignitaries were attending their end of term concert.

One of her colleagues, in the manner of a herald was supposed to declare as they were about to enter - "Hark! I hear the tramp of feet approaching." Instead in a fit of excitement and

OUR OLD HOUSE IN TEEBOY. THE WINDOW ON THE
SIDE WAS TO MY BEDROOM.
"THE LITTLE WINDOW WHERE THE SUN CAME
     PEEPING IN AT MOR'N".

nervousness exclaimed - "Hark! I hear the feet of tramps approaching" and thereby probably extinguished for all time any thoughts of a career on the stage!

Mother was an avid reader and would often indulge it by reading aloud on some favourite subject - a patriotic one. Many's the tale of derring do she related or perhaps some moral tale showing how a 'lost' person had recovered their dignity through prayer or abstinence from drink, which she equated with the first step on the slippery slope to perdition and ruin.

Her love of Ireland was unsurpassed and the fact that her generation had won independence for the twenty six counties was a source of great pride, but tinged with a great sadness by the memory of those who has suffered and fallen and that the six counties including our neighbouring country of Fermanagh a few miles away had been hived off and remained unfree.

She proudly kept my fathers medals and a pair of rosary beads sent to her from Crumlin Road jail by one of the Smiths who was under sentence of death there for the shooting of the R.I.C. policeman who had murdered the Lord Mayor of Cork - Thomas McCurtain. She was fanatical about education as an end in itself both as a teacher and a parent. She acted as a sort of unofficial shop steward for the area, harrying the county engineer to try and get the road repaired as well as tackling any company who tried to ride roughshod over any friend of neighbour, and many a pompous managing director felt the wrath of her pen.

Our parents married after the war of Independence but his uncle did not welcome him back, as some mischievous local had filled his imagination with thoughts of a young local beauty living in America who would return and marry him if he got rid of my father and had the house to himself. Of course there is no fool like an old fool when it comes to a young girl and he swallowed this story, hook, line and sinker. Father and Mother and their first son Paddy moved to Westmeath, raised their family and acquired a small farm.

The uncle meanwhile waited in vain for his Yankie femme fatale to arrive and one by one sold his cattle until the farm was no longer viable and it was put up for sale. Naturally my father was kept fully informed of the situation by some of his former neighbours while a few wrote to their relatives in America for the money to buy the land.

Uncle Hughie who lived in the home place in Aughaweena took a very direct approach to the problem and a few days before the sale he drove the cattle off, which had been put in to graze buchshee, by a fusillade of shots over their heads.

On the day of the sale, at the courthouse in Cavan, Hughie informed the potential purchasers that they were well aware who in fact should be the rightful owner and then calmly continued that anyone else who bid for the land would not go home alive. This had the desired effect, and there being no other bidder, my father purchased the property, where he had worked since boyhood.

Mother and all the youngsters moved back to Corlough with our furniture in a lorry, but my father walked his cattle all the way with the help of his two dogs, one of whom got killed along the way. It took him two days and two nights and he was physically exhausted when he arrived at his brothers home in Ardlougher. Although both parents were happy to be back in Cavan they really missed their neighbours and friends around Tang, Co Westmeath, and the memory of their young son Phillip buried in the graveyard near there.

Father missed his former locals - Maghera and the Three Jolly Pigeons, where as the song says "the three counties meet - Longford, Westmeath and Roscommon." He also missed his football friends - he played for Tubbercurry amongst others. I drove him up to Westmeath almost fifty years later and we went in for a drink to the "Pigeons" and the lady serving immediately recognised him!

Around Tang was a peaceful serene pastoral area, in "Goldsmith" country and their place lay between the Inny and the Shannon. Mum loved the villages, especially Glassan and visits to these and an odd trip to Mullingar were a delight to her. They never owned or drove a car but travelled in a trap, pulled, as Mum used to say "by a wild filly called Fan".

They were strong willed with definite ideas and consequently had their disagreements after one of which Dad went off to bed without joining in the rosary, which we always said as family each night when we were young. Mother took great delight that night in reciting the prayers extra loud and injected exclamations of "isn't it a shame for your father lying in bed without saying his prayers". These spats were never long lasting although my mother nearly always had the last word.

## 10

# *The Land Below The Mountains.*

Corlough stretched from the middle reaches of the Cuilcagh mountains down to our inland sea, Bunerky or as we called it Ardara lake. The whole area sloped at quite a steep angle from top to bottom so if you were cycling up to the chapel or post office from our position near the lake you had a very hard climb...but it was sheer heaven coming back as you barely had to peddle at all. Sideways the parish was bordered by Swanlinbar or Swad which started near Dernacrieve and by Corraleehan which started about halfway to Ballinamore.

It boasted a couple of rivers, in one of which salmon spawned, at least the ones which reached the beds having eluded the gaffs of James Eddie or any other of the two legged predators who appreciated the taste of the fish of knowledge, and led it to it's doom with a flashlight at the dead of night.

The top half of the parish was largely bog or rough grazing on which the owners kept large numbers of tough mountain sheep with the upper reaches held in commonage, that is each farmer could graze a number of sheep on the common land in proportion to the land they actually owned.

The people who lived in Corlough were nearly all small farmers who fought the thin soil for a living. 'Fought' is perhaps the wrong word because they seemed to have an almost mystical communion with the land which they loved with an intensity so that rows over land could last and did last for generations. They were quite prepared to fight and die for the land as those who over the centuries tried to take it from them found out. To this day to be labelled 'a land grabber' is the chief of the seven deadly sins.

There were at least five shops in the parish , two of which

doubled, as post offices and another as a pub. The populace were also served by two travelling shops. Michael Sweeney from Ballinamore owned and drove the travelling shop in our area and had his own advertising slogan on yellow packets of tea - "People who buy tea by chance, may, by chance, buy good tea, but people who take no chances buy Sweeneys' teas." We had four schools, Corratillan, Tullyveela, Tullybrack and Altahullion. We had two halls, Tonlegee and Corratillan, in which were held dances, bazaars and socials which provided the sum total of our entertainment, but the delights of the dances in particular was still in the future.

It was a common sight to see some of the sheep farmers setting off up the mountain in the morning, accompanied by a couple of border collie sheepdogs to check on and count their flocks who could roam all over the mountain and into Northern Ireland. They sold their sheep and wool in fairs both in and out of the 'jurisdiction' and nobody knew their income, turnover or profit. "A good few if you could count them" would be the nearest approximation they would admit to when asked how many they had. They also kept a few cows on the green fields which had been wrested from the bog and cleaned of stones over the millenia. These surrounded each house like little oases of green in the vast expanse of the brown heather bog.

The bog however was anything but a desert and supported a huge variety of wildlife with birds of all types, some of whom were really large like pheasants and grouse and their nemesis the fox, who also preyed on the populations of hares and rabbits. The ten-deep banks of top quality turf which covered most of the bog area was also a source of income to the owners who let a bank out for a season at a time.

The lower half of the parish - our half - down towards the lake was mixed farming; dairying and tillage with the milk being carted in ten gallon tanks to the local creamery in Templeport and returning with skim milk in the evenings to help feed the pigs.

The border with Northern Ireland or as we called it "the six counties" was only a few miles away and everyone followed events and incidents there with great interest.

THE BLUE HILLS OF BREFFNY.
WHEN THE CLOUDS AND SUN COMBINE THE
HILLS ARE A DEEP INDIGO BLUE.

Republican activists launched attacks on various military installations and one bomb which went off prematurely was clearly heard in our locality. The area had a long history of political tension and my Aunt Maggie often told me of a march by men and women from all around who hurried to Swanlinbar one Sunday in the early nineteen hundreds to prevent the chapel being burned by Orangemen. A song in recognition of this is still sung in the area and a verse tells of a certain Orangeman who obviously had strong feelings about the marchers;

"And Davy Knott broke up his pot and swore he'd kill them all....that low down crowd that marched from Ballinamore".

By all accounts several people were killed but the chapel survived. It is ironic that it was destroyed during the recent troubles probably by the political descendents of those who originally had intended to destroy it.

Ordinary crime was almost non-existent. We could and did leave our doors unlocked and no one would enter uninvited. If a robbery or such like occurred the Gardai would know who to interview, almost at once.

The crime that shook the whole area -a manslaughter - happened around New Year. A young man who was about to get married, his uncle, and his friend who was going to be best man had a row following a nights celebration and in the melee the prospective bridegroom fell, hit his head and died. The other two were tried and sent to prison for about ten years and on their release had to emigrate as no one would talk to them. The crime was the talk of the area for years because there had been no other comparable crime for ages.

The farmers fought an unrelenting war against water sodden fields and new drainage schemes were a regular feature as was attempts to eradicate rushes which certainly needed no fertiliser. But they succeeded with a mixture of stubbornness, pride and a noble belief in self sufficiency in raising large healthy families free of the pressures of the city and cocooned by a series of protective layers - family friends and the local community.

The people were a homogenous unit, with the same

standard of living, same problems, hopes and desires, and practically all of the same religion. Of course there were different political allegiances, Fianna Fail and Fine Gael - both based on the civil war divides, but it never intruded on the heart warming neighbourly concerns and mutual help which welled up like a supporting cushion when fate in her indiscriminate fashion laid a heavy hand on anyone.

Money was not present in great quantity, but neither was debt. Every farm and house was owned by its occupier. No mortgages or loans held a cold clammy grip over our hearth stones.

The old people had memories of the Wall Street crash and the great depression, closely followed by the trade war with Britain, when the latter imposed high tariffs on Irish Produce following De Valera's refusal to pay any further reparations. It was still fresh in their minds.

"If you owe them nothing they have no power over you " was their motto, and it stood them in good stead. They could walk with their heads held high and didn't need to doff their caps or bend their knee to bank manager or landlord. The monthly cheque from the creamery took care of the day to day necessities and the large sums received on the sale of the calves, pigs or dry cattle were the reservoirs for the purchase of new clothes, shoes, stock or equipment. These two types of income, both regular and delayed suited the pace of our life and temperament and the tenor of the times. It is something the architects of modernisation with their commitment to playing the global village theme of economics would do well not to scorn - but to reflect on the strong, sturdy, sons of the soil that lost era of self sufficiency and self reliance produced.

No amount of computer literacy can emulate the small farmer scenario and when the giant international corporation, who always arrives with extravagant promises and many photo opportunities decides to restructure, or in reality move their manufacturing plant to the latest part of the global village whose slave labour rates of pay will boost their profits, what will replace it. The answer cannot be to cover vast areas of productive land with millions of pines. They were touted as a future salvation but

THE LAND AND LAKES BELOW THE MOUNTAIN.

they have not and will not produce jobs at local level. The foresters promised an abundance of jobs but now when after fifteen or twenty years the trees are ready for harvesting there is only one worker operating a computerised tractor.

The strength and cohesion of the locality can only be maintained by utilising the land in the manner to which it is suited and this will nearly always be in a self sufficiency situation, producing quality not mass produced food and ensuring that the sounds of nature, the dawn chorus, the cuckoo, the corncrake and the bitterns cry are joined by human voices in talk or song and that our countryside is not reduced to a human free zone. Where at the diktat of "An Taisce" the country people will not be allowed to build a house in case it might possibly interfere with the enjoyment of the landscape by visitors as they cycle by !

Hopefully the parish will see a resurgence in numbers and there are some encouraging signs. As people become more and more fed up with the pressures of city life, the lack of friendliness, the violence and crime and the realisation that cities and towns are not the best environment to bring up children or for that matter to grow old in, the desire to move back to the less populated areas will grow stronger and a number who can, will take the step. It can seem like a backward step at first but when you calmly consider that the high income you can achieve in the city has to be spent in order to maintain that artificial lifestyle and that there is precious little left at the end of the month anyway, what is the point?

Might it not be better to break the chains that bind, the large mortgages practically for life, the expenses, the hours spent in traffic jams and with one leap be free?

It may be time to admit that our parents and grandparents were a lot cleverer than we were, and that far from living in a restricted manner owing to lack of ambition they had summed up the pros and cons and chosen the better option.

A lot of "the media" scoff at a former Taoiseach's dream of young men playing Gaelic sports and Colleens dancing at the crossroads but it is a nobler aspiration than piling them into high rise and high density apartments and watching the resultant chaos that ensues.

# 11

## *Fairs and Sports.*

Fairs or sales of cattle, horses, donkeys, sheep, pigs, fowl and produce on the streets or fair greens of the local towns and villages were the power surges of the local economy. They were as old as the Celtic way of life - an integral part of the livelihood of the people since our days on the Anatolian plains before our horse based society stormed its way through Europe to its final resting home on the wild Atlantic shores. From time immemorial, Celts calculated their wealth by the numbers and quality of their cattle and horses, and the reverence for these animals still burns brightly as anyone who attends a race meeting or a mart can testify.

The work started in the dark of early morn, with the men driving their horses and carts, or dressed in strong hob-nailed boots with ash plants or stout blackthorn sticks driving their cattle anything up to seven or eight miles on foot.

But the fair was a film set and everyone an actor and each had a good part. It was full of sound, colour and excitement. Each fair had its special reputation - one was best for bullocks, another noted for horses or pigs and yet another might be excellent for sheep. The fair green fairly throbbed with cattle awaiting new owners, just like the stockades in the cowboy films. The carts were unhitched and backed against the pavements to display their loads of potatoes, cabbage, lettuce, turnips and onions. Some had closed-in crates housing chickens, hens, cockerels, ducks, geese and turkeys. Some had crates of young pigs, bonhams or maybe calves.

Ruddy faced farmers strode back and forth, slapped hands as big as shovels, while a supposedly neutral third party kept them together until the bargain was clinched, and the buyer transferred

74

a quantity of well worn notes from a large pad in his back pocket to the seller who in turn had to return a certain amount or luckpenny back to the buyer to show that he wished him all success with the purchase and had not cast an evil eye over the animal he had just sold. And now of course both buyer and seller had to adjourn to the nearest hostelry to treat the dealmaker and themselves.

The fair was the best thing the towns' shopkeepers could hope for, it was manna from heaven. Plenty of money changing hands, the streets full of people and all in a spending mood. The pubs were doing a roaring trade with hot whiskies, guinness and port being very acceptable. The tailors' tapemeasures were negotiating ample waists and rumps for suits ordered by customers flush with the money from their sales, and shoe shops and 'eating houses' were getting their share. Even the dentist would visit the town for the day and deal with a few roots who were succumbing to the passage of time...and I have no doubt that a blow or two from a blackthorn stick necessitated a visit to the doctor.

Not everybody at the fair was interested in buying or selling. It was just too good an excuse to escape into town for a good days carousing, and many a man who was not ready to buy or sell any of his stock informed his wife with due solemnity that it was of utmost importance for him to be at the fair "to see how things were going".

Some women attended the fairs and many a drapers shop had its turnover dramatically increased by wives capturing their husbands, financially speaking, at a weak but opportune moment as their back pockets were full from the sale of a beast.

Fairs could bring simmering tensions to the fore and in the old days 'faction fighting' was rife between groups of different persuasions or indeed of no persuasion at all. Agricultural, Political and Sectarian secret societies all had their adherents, and many a head was broken in the name of such as the "Molly Maguires, Ribbonmen, Peep-o-Day boys, Defenders, Parnellites, Anti-Parnellites, and after the civil war Pro and Anti treaty groups. But most fights were just for "the hang" of it, and indeed there were some champions who could be said to be professional...

yes, prize fighters in a code of their own. There was a very strong local tradition of stick fighting and up to the 1970s a local man dressed in Fairisle jumper, trousers tucked into his socks, wearing his hob-nailed boots and with his blackthorn stick resting on his shoulder would stroll up and down the main street of Ballyconnell looking for any potential challenger to his crown.

The authorities, religious and secular, frowned on this form of entertainment but contests, accompanied by heavy betting were a frequent occurance at a natural amphitheatre a few miles outside Ballyconnell, at Ballyheady.

*"At Ballyheady, near Fartrin Cross - a lonesome stretch of ground,*

*that once was famous for fighting - the murderin' hollow is found.*

*Now it once was Croke Park for stick fightin' and no man was a warrior crowned,*

*Till he'd stood in the murderin' hollow and battered his man to the ground.*

*We were raised on a hill near Ardlougher and oft' on the nights of the fair,*

*The shouts and the thump of the blackthorn could be heard on the quiet night air,*

*We knew all the names of the fighters, we knew every parry and call,*

*And we knew that the Bully Malowney was the greatest stick fighter of all.*

*Famous men came long journeys to fight him, and the hollow 'ed be thronged of a night,*

*When word got around some contender was to give the old Bully a fight.*

*One crowd came up from Fermanagh, with a sidecar and two waggonettes,*

*They'ed a hero to vanquish the Bully, aye ,and sovereigns to cover their bets.*

*A strong cruel fighter this Nolan. He'd once killed a man near Augnacloy,*

*But the Bully just lathered that keeboy like a schoolmaster beating a boy.*

*I remember, mind we were just children, I remember the night of it yet,*

*When the uncles burst into the kitchen and announced that the bully was beat.*

*He had beaten this Pheilim Maguire in a long gruelling fight last July,*

*But that night, and no doubt it - he'd met with his master that night.*

*For the bulk of a week no one saw him - then on Friday he came to the shop,*

*Picked up his tea and some sugar, spoke to no one and didn't stop.*

*You remember them yellow stamped postcards-people wrote on a lot in those days,*

*There was one in the post-box that evening and everyone wondered what he'd to say,*

*To his son the young Bully near Glasgow - 'twas only a bit of a note,*

*In letters as big as your thumbnail-"COME HOME DADDY WANTS YOU" was wrote.*

*Now six months or maybe a year later-there broad as the butt of a tree,*

*In the doorway stood the young Bully - "You were wanting me Daddy" says he.*

*"I was, can you fight?" says the father - "If you can than I've got you a job"*

*And without even waiting an answer, he hit him a puck in the gob.*

*Now the young man reacted like lightning with a punch like the kick of a mule,*

*And the ould man went down in the corner, and the table was brook, aye and the stool,*

*And he sat there 'midst the plates and the sugar for a moment before he came-too,*

*Then he smiled his grim smile and he said "Aye gossun-you'll do".*

*Now Father Brady was dead against factions and he tipped off Inspector McCoy,*

*And had constables brought from Belturbet and a serjeant and men from Bawnboy.*

He read out the whole thing from the Altar as a shame and a crying Disgrace,

Yet hundreds turned up at Drumreilly where they thought that the fight would take place.

But the serjeant was watching Maguire and he saw that he carried no stick,

And he watched him stroll off down the Mass-track , but sure 'twas only a trick,

At the kesh near the mearin at Prunty's stood a group of men , Friends of Maguire,

And there on his own sat the Bully , on a stone at the end of the byre.

There was silence and no introductions-there was silence and not a man spoke,

As the men faced each other in the paddock, Maguire----he made the first stroke.

Then by Heaven - there was murder in Gaelic - as blows poured from left and from right,

There's ould men will swear by the bible that never was seen such a fight.

For thirty minutes hard at it, then without any signal at all,

Maguire swung back to his cronies and Malowney went back to the wall.

Five minutes rest - then up boys and at it,

Now the blood was beginning to flow, for the blows were still cruel and vicious,

Though the pace was beginning to slow.

Then Malowney he made his big gamble, for a moment he lowered his guard,

but Maguire was too slow to take it.

And the Bully he played his trump card.

The great too-handed stroke of his father - it had finished off many a round

And it came crashing down on Maguire and he sank like a sack to the ground.

Now you might think that that was the end of it-but it wasn't.

In Drumreilly at Mass the next Sunday Father Brady was at it again,

*And he read out both the Bully and Pheilim as sinful and violent
men.
Then up with a roar jumps the Bully saying I never expected to be
here back in my own native Parish to be read off the Altar said he.
And he stamped to the door with his hat on but he paused there
before he went through,*
*And he looked the whole length of the Chapel and he let out a
mighty yahoo."*
*AND THAT WAS THE LAST THAT WAS SEEN OR HEARD OF
HIM AROUND DRUMREILLY.*

The vast majority of fairs were peaceable get togethers,
where business was conducted in the time honoured manner, on a
face to face basis where old friendships were renewed and
consolidated without any hint of trouble. But needless to say there
were many disagreements over the purchase or sales in the course
of a "fairday", where a man might incur financial loss and ridicule
if he was sold a pup or as would more likely be said "he was sold a
pig in a poke". His opinions would not be given as much weight
from then on and every Tom, Dick or Harry would be trying to get
one over on him, and his life would not be easy in the future.

My father-in-law, Eugene O'Sullivan, often told me of his
experience of a fair in Cappawhite, many miles to the south. It
seems a disagreement broke out over the sale of a heifer - the seller
claiming that the animal was a good two year old and the
purchaser, shortly after the deal was completed, coming to the
conclusion that the animal was a poor three year old. The backers
of each protagonist proceeded to manufacture a riot which needed
the intervention of vast numbers of Gardai and a substantial
number of military to quell.

For up to twenty years later a mischief maker had only to
go into a pub in Cappawhite and say "She was definitely a two year
old ", to cause the shennanigans to start all over again.

But the demise of the fair was a sad development both for
the town merchants and the farmers. It robbed the locality of a
fantastic day of colour, banter and interaction - a spectacle older
than recorded history was consigned to the dustbins of memory. It
deprived the pubs, shopkeepers and eating houses of a significant

portion of their income, and it placed a barrier between the buyer and seller and replaced it with the marts with their ordered production line methods.

From then on no money changed hands on the day of the sale - no longer were the buyer and seller to be seen slapping each others hands and returning the luckpennies, and now of course your business was no longer private, now a paper trail existed for every bureaucratic busybody to poke his nose into your affairs.

The way was being made ready for the parasites of modern time, the taxmen and vatmen, who producing nothing themselves, strive harder and harder to extract evermore from those who do.

Sunday was the great day of relaxation and enjoyment. Saturday night was not then the chief entertainment night. "You should be at home polishing your shoes" was often the putdown to any teenage inclination to roam on that night. But come Sunday, once you had done your duty, and made sure the animals were looked after the remainder of the day and a large portion of the night were yours to enjoy. Not for us the dour Calvinistic observance or brooding melancholy of a rigid approach to Christianity. It was our day off and we were going to make the most of it and it was on Sundays that all sports meetings were held.

A sports day was held once a year in Ballyconnell and Ballinamore but it was the day one was held in Feehans field that really sticks in my memory. Glorious sunshine prevailed and there was a very full list of events. Football, High and Long jumping, and running were all available but it was the horse-racing which provided the best excitement and sport. Nearly every house had a horse in those days and the race was taken very seriously. Byrnes mare, who was being ridden by one of the Farrell Dolans veered off the course and off out the Bull lane and John James Smith, who came third, claimed that he was actually holding his mare back as he thought there was another circuit of the field to go !

The days' outdoor activities ended with a seven-a-side football tournament between five or six of the local parishes, and the whole thing was rounded off with a Ceili and Old Time dance in Tonlegee hall.

The local and county towns held show days, sometimes in

conjunction with the local agricultural societies. Cattle, Horse and Sheep judging were the main activities but there were also some show jumping, donkey races and the usual fairground attractions.

Many years later at the showgrounds in Cavan town was the only place I have even seen a certain game being "won" by a participant. This was the competition where a pound note was wrapped around a wooden peg and held by a rubber band. A rope fence surrounded the tent to keep the participants a certain distance from the pegs and the idea was to throw a ring which had to go over the peg and settle down evenly round the base. It was to all intents and purposes impossible to do this as the ring was barely able to fit over the peg.

There were a couple of hundred of us out at the show from the college and a large number surrounded this particular tent and while some distracted the attendant a thrower slipped under the rope and put the ring firmly into position before scampering back. The tent owners face was a picture to behold when he turned back and saw the ring in position. He knew it was impossible but with the number of us present he had to pay up, and from then on he only allowed one person to throw at a time and kept his eyes peeled to the action, and nothing could induce him to turn away and provide a further opportunity for our winning method.

Some of the shows might have up to a hundred stalls with all types of merchandise ranging from farm produce to clothes and anything in between, and for many families it was the outing of the year, or at least deserved a new bonnet for every female attending and a general spruce up for the menfolk as well.

One of the chief points of interest was the displays of farm machinery, old and new, and many a hand was lovingly rubbed over the latest models, which might have to wait a few more years before sufficient funds would be available to acquire them.

## 12

## *Dances.*

My very first dance was at Lavey Strand Carnival. It was on a Sunday afternoon and thirty or forty miles from home. I was about thirteen at the time and had been sent to Carrickmacross to sit a scholarship examination and had taken lodgings at a boarding house in the town whose clientele were salesmen. As I was so young they took me under their wing and one of them, a salesman for HB ice cream had had a very bad week. It had rained everyday and no one needed fresh supplies of ice cream. But he was certainly resourceful and managed to rent a space in the marquee at Lavey Strand, so called because it boasted a lake shore, on the Sunday, and as I had no examinations that day he brought me along to help.

He managed to sell all his stock, and at retail rather than wholesale prices, and after a stint selling ice cream, I was free to sample the delights of the dance hall and with a couple of quid in my pocket for my labours.

I never looked back.

Lavey was too far away for a return visit as our only means of transport was a bicycle I had to share with Enda, so I turned my attention to our local hotspot, Corlough's very own Eldorado...Tonlegee. Built of galvanized sheeting, it boasted a stage, a dancing area of about 40 x 20 feet with forms at each side for seating the patrons - the men on the left and the ladies on the right. There was a cloakroom on the left of the stage and the windows were wooden...but none of this mattered one jot. This was where it was all happening, and we were determined to savour it to the full.

Sunday night was THE night. The football, fishing and

milking were all finished that bit earlier - our production rate speeded up considerably, and we were brylcreemed and brilliantined in good time. Enda and I had only one bike between us and as we couldn't cut it in two, we did the next best thing...we divided the journey! One cycled as far as Phil Thomas's cross, left the bicycle and whichever of us had walked the first half now cycled the second half, and we both arrived at Tonlegee at roughly the same time.

There was always a dozen or two milling around outside, and some of them never went in at all. "I've got a bit of a cough, ahem ahem" was John James Martin's excuse but really he was afraid of the ribbing he would get from the latchykokes if he went in, and preferred to stay in the safety of the darkness outside.

When you paid your schilling, or one and sixpence to Patrick Reilly or Hotyeen or Patrick Nuckey as his nicknames went, you were transported to our idea of Shangri La, and for one night in the seven you could believe that your wildest fantasies might come true.

The hall seethed with life. Girls in gingham dresses, or skirts and blouses and the obligatory high heels, their hair in beehives or in long tresses down to their waists, sat on the far form or stood in groups near it , giving their verdicts on each male as he came through the door. The young men and those not so young, but still hoping as they said, congregated on the opposite side, a small number in suits , some in trousers and sports coats and a lot in jumpers instead of jackets. They jostled about eyeing the girls while pretending that it was the last thing in the world on their minds.

The Silver Star Dance Band or McNamara's Ceili Band would be on stage tuning up and the hall was lit by three Tilley or Aladdin lamps hanging from the rafters.

The first dance would be called - a set piece..."The Haymakers Jig" or "The Siege of Ennis" to get the crowd going. This was sound psychology as the boys didn't need to have dutch courage to ask the girls, and they for their part were not too worried who had asked them as being a set they didn't actually have to dance with them on a one-to-one basis. Everyone knew the steps to these two dances, and even if you weren't sure you could

MARGARET'S CROSS, COALOUGH. SITE OF THE
UNFORTUNATE ATTEMPT BY 'S' TO CARRY
HIS BELOVED TO THE DANCE BY HORSE.

always improvise or follow the leader. Great to-ing and fro-ing was the order of the day, with an additional flourish of a swing to get the blood up...and if you could swing the girl completely off her feet your status as an expert was established.

These dances went under the description of "Ceile and Oldtime" and after the first set the band would play a few slower dances where you could really get in close if you could get the right partner. This set the pattern for the night and most nights you would hear the same songs and tunes repeated several times. "By special request we are having this number again..." the band singer would announce, and one night I heard "Pick me up on your way down" five or six times! At any rate I was able to hum it from then on.

The men signalled to the girls in some covert way, like a wink or a nod , in fact the more hidden the method of asking the better, as the greatest dread was in losing face. The man was destroyed for life who walked across the hall, in full view of everyone and got refused. He would have to retreat with loud guffaws of mockery ringing in his ears and as they said wouldn't do any good from then on...at least not that night. In most cases girls would dance with anyone who asked them as to refuse too often would get them the title of a "stuck up old so and so ", but now and again they would hang out in the hope of a better deal, especially if they saw someone they really fancied making a move in their direction. The best refusal I ever heard was the one allegedly given by a girl from Manchester "Dance with my mate...I'm sweating".

The "ladies choice" dance reversed the roles and were the making or breaking of many an embryonic romance. Of course this golden opportunity for playing a nasty trick on some poor benighted soul was not lost on the wide boys and sometimes, with the girls connivance some poor old devil who had no hope in the world was singled out by some femme fatale only to be mocked and derided by all 'in the know', and be severely disappointed when his heightened ardour persuaded him to try to soar out of his allotted orbit in the constellation of Tonlegee.

A sharp eyed observer of people would have seen and noted the tactics employed in this never ending game of the human mating ritual. The peacock may display his beautiful plumage to

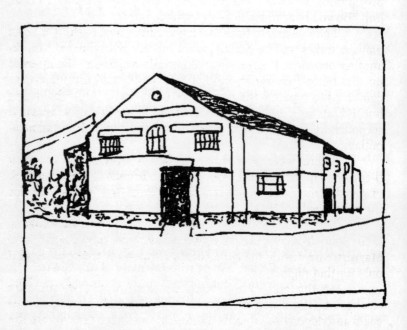

WONDERLAND BALLROOM, BAWNBOY.

impress the female of the species but Petey the Garrier employed the latest technology to attract the object of his desires. He had found a dancing partner and as he foxtrotted around the hall, he continually lifted and stretched his left arm to display his version of the peacock's plumage---his newly acquired wristwatch but his female partner either genuinely or deliberately refused to take notice. After numerous attempts Petey could stand it no longer and in desperation pushed the watch up to her ear while proclaiming in a voice loud enough to be clearly heard by all near him "Do you hear the whick-whack of de boy?"

,Petey seems to have had a bad run of luck in the Tonlegee maiden stakes and he berated cruel fortune who cheated him on another occasion. It seems he successfully negotiated the internal hurdles but on emerging with his lady the fog and utter darkness combined to separate them never to be reunited. "And what harm but I'd already bought de chocolates!" was Petey's resigned response to a lost courting opportunity and a pointless financial outlay.

There were a number of males who never involved themselves in the female chase, probably through shyness and lack of social ability, but as one sage put it "Sure that leaves more for the rest of us."

One of the bands who played in Tonlegee was McNamaras' Ceili Band from Cavan town, and their lead singer was Sadie Maguire who during the bands break became my first girlfriend if only for that night.

At the end of the night someone would go into the cloakroom (there was no light there),  and gather an armful of coats and deposit them in the middle of the dance floor where the owners picked out their own.

There were similar halls a few miles around - Drumbrick, Swanlinbar and the Workhouse hall in Bawn, and bicycles permitting, we did the rounds depending on which bands were playing. And if they attracted a big crowd so much the better, as everyone seemed to function much better and without reserve if packed as close as sardines.

But the day of halls such a Tonlegee were drawing to a close. The Star Ballroom in Ballyconnell was doing a roaring trade and Ben Barney had arrived home from America, bought a pub and built the Wonderland Ballroom next door. Our horizons were widening, the bands were bigger, the floors were now of Canadian maple which swung up and down slightly with the crowds and the prizes juicier or so it seemed. Coaches were bringing girls from Cavan and Enniskillen, and to us it seemed that these places were definitely of the ilk of Sodom and Gomorrah. Then with any luck at all, these girls would be Jezebbels, one and all.

It was no use trying to share a bicycle to these far flung outposts, at least seven miles in the case of the Star and cavalry detachments of equal opportunity proportions would glide down the Marsh road, pass through Bawn at high speed and converge on Wonderland or the Star. Our transports joined the rows of bicycles along the hedges. Fashions were changing. The Teddy Boy era was emerging overseas and although we never wholly adopted the style, we did make certain adjustments and mine was a yellow shirt with turned up collar. It might be freezing cats and dogs or doing horrible things to the anatomy of brass monkeys, but it wasn't the done thing to wrap yourself up as if you felt the cold. No...you had to breast it out, although one or two sneakily wore a light jumper under their shirts to combat the cold , at least on the journey to and fro.

These halls cost a lot to enter but the bands were much larger and professional and travelled the length and breath of the country. The Clipper Carlton from Strabane were first in the field, closely followed by Brendan Bowyer and The Royal from Waterford, The Dixies from Cork, Johnny Flynn from Tuam, The Black Aces from Kilkenny, The Melody Aces, and The Mighty Avons from Cavan and then the king Big Tom and the Mainliners from Castleblayney. Our local area had its own representatives in the big time, The Derrylin Starlight Band and The Golden Eagles. Country and Western ruled the roost in the new halls with a smattering of ballads and certain numbers in the style of the big swing bands, all dressed in smart suits or blazers and trousers, and white shirts with perhaps the lead singer dressed all in white.

The dances changed too. This was the era of Rock and Roll. Bill Hailey and his Comets had come to Derry and it ended with teenagers dancing on the roof of cars. We had no cars to

THE STAR, BALLYCONNELL.

dance on but between jiving to the sounds of Bill Hailey and twisting to Chubby Checker, we wore out our shoes, and after a half hour or so the cute fellow with the hidden jumper under his shirt was now wishing he had braved the cold elements outside rather than the soaring temperature inside. But were we complaining...? Certainly not. We had reached the happy state of Nirvana. We had a far greater choice - we weren't known and skirts were becoming shorter.

We even ventured thirty or forty miles from home. A few vehicles had appeared in the locality - Byrne's brown Commer van being one, and fifteen of us piled into it now and again on special occasions such as St. Stephens night and New years eve - for two shillings or half a crown we travelled in style. It only added to the excitement when on one New years eve the lights would not work and I had to light the way with a flashlamp held out the passenger window. On our longer trips to Roosky on the Leitrim/Roscommon border we were well and truly far from home and could give unfettered rein to our imagination when telling the girls our occupations.

"John" was earnestly explaining the pressures of being in charge of Aer Lingus's wonderful flying machines to an awe struck young maiden when Pee Mc...destroyed his whole technique by requesting the loan of his donkey to carry out turf in the bog the following morning, but the most disastrous effort I heard was the chat up line from a young farmer who also worked for the recently established Bovine Artificial Insemination Board. His romantic endeavours fell completely flat when he breathlessly stammered out to a nubile young thing "I am a big farmer and a bull as well."

The first time I ever did the 'Twist' was completely by accident. I was negotiating round Wonderland with my own version of a foxtrot when I got cornered, boxed in or imprisoned in a welter of gyrating arms and legs and there and then to avoid utter humiliation at my inability to proceed, I had to take my cue from Chubby Checker.

The Twist took the place by storm for months and the two best exponents of the dance, Paddy Kilfeather and Norah McGovern even made it to the final of a competition in Bundoran where the first prize was a car...an unbelievable prize at that time.

TONLEGEE HALL — OUR GALVANIZED EL DORADO.

On Sunday night, the ditches along the road from Wonderland in both directions would be lined with bicycles and the few people who had cars would park beside the hall.

These new style halls such as Wonderland, Lakeland, the Sports Centre, The Maple and Roosky were all strictly teetotal and the strongest beverage available was a lemonade or an orange juice but it didn't seem to hamper our enjoyment in any way. I 'm sure some of the more mature patrons probably had a jar or two or maybe a drop of poteen before arriving, but generally the dancing scene was alcohol free and certainly free from any other stimulants as well.

Many of the men had distinctive styles of dancing, a swing of the shoulders or a quick twirl was employed to show off their ability and confidence while the less artistic moved along set lines and might even have difficulty turning the corners. One couple, who had been schooled in the art of dancing, were an occasion of great mirth and derision through utter jealousy on our part. I can still hear the sound of one of the 'Johnny Ellens' pounding the floor during "The siege of Ennis", whils't a stone , rattled down the tin roof , thrown by one of the 'Hardy Annuals' on permanent duty outside.

Tonlegee doubled as a cinema and films or pictures as we called them were shown usually on a Thursday night. They were nearly always cowboy films - Hopalong Cassidy or Rip Kirby starring in films with names like 'The bushwhacker of Dry Gulch Creek'. The screen was a white sheet hung on the bottom wall and the projector was powered by a generator positioned on the street outside. The great problem was getting the generator to start as the workings were often wet, but no matter how long it took we were quite happy as soon as we saw the fearless horsemen careering across the screen, six-guns blazing, vanquishing the baddies. They also showed films in the 'Star' in Ballyconnell and I remember watching a gangster film there. There was no doubt whatsoever which of the characters were the baddies as they all had long scars down their faces to ensure identification and the patrons actually stood up and clapped when the FBI caught them.

A few yards down from Tonlegee was Devines cross and it was the setting for the open air dances on Sunday evenings during

OUR SUMMERTIME OPEN AIR DANCING VENUE.

the Summer. Music was provided either by a violinist or accordian player or sometimes both would play as we danced our cares away on the tarred road. Many's the evening old Pat Quinn, who was over eighty at the time, while walking home from his afternoon pints in Feehans, would stop and give a rendition of "The valley of Knockinure."

"And the banshee cried, when her Fenians died,
In the valley of Knockinure.."
All ten or twelve verses of it.

It was at an open air Ceile at Devines cross that I heard my very first political speech, on behalf of Sinn Fein, by a man from down the Swanlinbar road, called Pat Duffy and when he referred to the then British Ambassador - a certain Mr.Clutterbuck - everyone had a great laugh...not at all what Pat had in mind.

## 13

# *Earthly Characters in our Pantomime.*

James was a renowned one. He was an intelligent man, a master builder but he also had a naivety and inclination for plain talking which would have made him an excellent 'straight' man in a comedy duo like Morecombe and Wise without even trying.

His talks with a local romeo called 'M' provided much mirth.

### Scene 1

James gives a lift to a lady from further up the country who had taken a bus as far as Bawnboy on her way to visit 'M'.

She openly stated her destination, against all the rules of local discretion and thus gave the game away on 'M'.

She played the game a little further and pretending to be all coquettish and vulnerable - "a young lady could be interfered with along these lonely country lanes." James, without the slightest sense of irony related the story as follows;

"Ah I said, my good woman (indeed like myself she was well past her sell by date) you have no reason at all to worry on that account."

### Scene 2

Cullens pub in Swanlinbar.

The occasion was pre-funeral night drinks. Present - Enda, James and 'M'. The latter delayed going in until James had ordered a round. Then Enda got the next round and now 'M' excused himself and went to the toilet so that James had to order a third round. This was all part of a game or ritual and did not reflect any desire not to buy a round on 'M's part. Indeed he would more than make up for it before the night was over.

"James why did you never get married?" 'M' enquired, "and you having a good house and a bathroom...the women love a nice bathroom."

"Dammy I don't know" said James, "but I once was going to meet a girl in Fenaghville, even though the Priest had said on Sunday that it was a sin to go there as they kept the dances going to two AM instead of closing at twelve midnight as every other hall did. Well, I cycled there with Phil McKiernan but when we got to Fenaghville there was a big black cloud over the hall which we thought was the devil and we turned and cycled home as fast as we could."

"It would take more than a black cloud to make me turn back" replied 'M'.

At this stage he produces a little black book (honestly) from his inside pocket saying "Well I always like to help those who cannot help themselves in the women department. Now there's this woman in Dowra who would suit you down to the ground and maybe Enda would give us a run out to meet her one night?"

James, however was under no illusion that he was God's gift to womankind, and if M was so certain that she would be favourably disposed to him then there must be a big catch somewhere, and with his usual plain talking, down-to-earth manner, broached the question "Whats wrong with her M ?"

Without hesitation - "Nothing...she's perfect" was the reply in a tone which announced he knew that several more pints would be winding their way to him before the night was out.


'S' who lived in the upper reaches of the parish was a friend of James. They had known each other since God was a gossun. Although not a big man, 'S' was very strong and prepared to tackle any problem with fearless determination.

He once cycled down all the way to Howdens wood mill with a large ironshod cart wheel round his neck, forcing cars and lorries to give way. "I know they were heavily loaded but I was heavily loaded myself" was his comment. He once cycled back from the fair in Dowra with an unwilling and uncooperative ram tethered to the back of the bicycle. The ram's tactics alternated between digging his heels in and bringing the whole charabanc to a sudden and painful halt, or charging 'S' at his most vulnerable.

But my favourite one relates to the time he was taking a girl to a dance in Drumbrick. He had arranged to meet her near Margaret's cross, a couple of hundred yards above the chapel. In the nature of things nothing ever remained secret for long in Corlough so a small group of the likely lads had assembled there to watch the proceedings.

His date duly arrived but there was a problem because 'S's mode of transport was not a car, van, tractor or bicycle...but a horse! 'S'dismounted from his charger like a knight of old and brought the horse closely in along the ditch so his 'amour' could stand on it and climb onto the horse's back, but true love does not run smoothly. As 'S' held the horses's head in close, it would move out its hind quarters so the lady could not mount, and when he would go around to push its hind quarters in to the ditch, it would move its front half, its head and shoulders out.

The problem would have surely defeated a lesser man who might have had to enlist help from one of the sneering onlookers, and in hindsight it would have been better. But not our Sir Lancelot. After several fruitless attempts, 'S' in desperation made one superhuman effort, he lifted the lady high above his head and placed her on the horse's back but in doing so he had dropped the reins. His woes were just commencing.

The horse took off like the wind before 'S'could grasp the reins and galloped off down the road with the young lady hanging on for dear life and issuing alternative heart wrenching appeals for help and blood curdling threats of the retribution to follow. 'S' was doing a fair representation of an Olympic sprinter while imploring the girl to hold on, and the horse to stop in that order and in the same breath.

It did stop...not gradually but suddenly when confronted by a cyclist coming round a corner and 'S's ' lady flew through the air and landed in a drain of rust coloured, stagnant spa water. 'S' was still running down the road cursing the animal and praying that his love was still alive. She meanwhile had surfaced, climbed out of the drain, unrecognisable as the dance goer of a few minutes ago. She strode up to 'S', gave him a resounding slap across the face and thus ended a budding romance despite his last desperate throw of the dice; "There's no need to take it like that!"

Paddy "Clark" had been a very good dancer in his youth, according to local wisdom. "He had a great bit of speed to him" was the acknowledged verdict but whether speed equated with gracefulness is anybody's guess.

He had many tales collected during an eventfull life but my favourite was a story he told with zest of an incident which occurred during a spell he spent in a psychiatric hospital in Monaghan, owing to his fondness for the bottle!

I'll let him tell it in his own words :

"I was allowed out each day and used to go to a pub in the Diamond. One of the people with me in the hospital was a fellow - a dwarf - who used to perform in Duffy's circus. I used to put on bets for him and one day he won a few quid. When he got the money he asked me to bring in a half bottle of whiskey so I did and half an hour later you could hear all this shouting and roaring and it took four men to hold the dwarf down."

Paddy was a very generous man and his pension took a fair old hammering on a Thursday and Friday, and I recall him coming back from one such expedition, dragging his shopping bag behind him up the Corneen road with a long trail behind - the result of the broken eggs at the bottom. Mick used to cut his hair and toe nails. I met the latter one day as he was setting off on this errand.

"I hope he has plenty of hot water ready as his nails are like horse's hoofs...the last time I cut his hair he ran out squealing like a pig." No wonder...Mick's hairdressing tool was a horse clipper which used to belong to George Donohue and in a careless moment he had made quite an inroad into the flesh above Paddy's ear!

Court day in Ballyconnell usually threw up the usual list of suspects supplemented by the possible appearance of a publican for allowing late drinking, maybe a customer of his for imbibing too much or maybe the sheepish looking protagonists in some row, nearly always involving a few cuffs around the ears or a bloody nose rather than a dangerous affray.

Of course human nature being what it is it was the taking down of some respected citizen, especially one who in the general opinion thought too much of himself which generated most excitement and glee, mostly secret, from the drinking fraternity.

If you were a hardworking solid type who was out tending to his business during the day you could wait until the weekend and read the reports in 'The Anglo Celt' about all the unfortunates who had been "brought up the steps"as being summoned to court was known locally. But heck, where was the fun in that? Brendan Magee always attended the court, once or twice at the request of the Judiciary where he would defend himself with great eloquence and wit but mostly he was there in his role as observer and freelance reporter for the clientele of McBarrons pub.

Brendan would get in early, acquire a good viewing and listening seat and write it all down - the charges, evidence and the verdicts on a large sheet of brown paper in pencil. He was back in the pub before the good judge had got "down the steps" himself and regaled all with the ins and outs of the days proceedings.

Brendan used to be a poultry buyer and still plied his former trade around Christmas time when the turkey trade was in full swing. Unfortunately the five barrels of plucked down and feathers were left uncovered and a brisk breeze blowing across the Woodford canal lifted the turkeys' former clothing and deposited them over the town as a winter's coat of snow.

Michael had received several gifts for Christmas and he listed them religiously, ending up with one accompanied by as he said "a lovely card of The Wolfe Tones."

He handed it to me and as I stared at it incredulously he enquired "It is The Wolfe Tones isn't it?"

I said "no Michael it's The Three Wise Men".

He was indignant and shouted "That's the last time that H... in Ballyconnell reads my letters". It will probably come as somewhat of a surprise to Warfield & Co to discover that they have been canonised!

The Cawley brothers, Mick and Tom from near Bawnboy, made the daily trip to Ballyconnell on their tractor. Mick did the driving and Tom sat on the back, above the linkbox directing all traffic to pass whether the road was clear or not.

They famously once overturned on their homeward journey into Papie's garden and stayed there with the wheels still turning and Tom complaining to Mick about the length of time it was taking to reach home.

They sometimes gave Michael a lift, standing on the linkbox although he swore that they tried to kill him once when the driver Mick suddenly dropped the linkbox down on the road and Michael rolled down Hendersons hill closely followed by a full bottle of Calor gas.

On another occasion they rounded the corner and headed out of town oblivious to the fact that they had pulled the wing off a car parked near the junction. The Gardai duly caught up with them on the aforementioned Hendersons hill , arrested the Cawleys and sent Michael walking home. Of course when the local boyos heard of it, they spiced it up and added several possible scenarios of what the eventual outcome was likely to be, including a possible "trip up the steps". They convinced Michael of this and he informed me a few days later "Its all over the Woodford...they are going to charge the Cawleys with dangerous driving and me with directing traffic from the rear!"

One of my favourite stories concerning Michael was the time he purchased a discounted tin of paint for his chimneys and piers. He got a neighbour to paint the chimneys and did the piers himself. Unfortunately the colour was pink and a few days later when I was passing he was furiously scrubbing it off the piers. He explained that on pension day when he visited a few hostelries in the town "everyone joined in singing 'Lily the Pink'."


I do not remember Cloakie but I did pick blackberries from around the ruins of his house and got four shillings and sixpence per stone for them from Tommy Ball.

Cloakie got his name from the martial cloak which was his trademark. He was very proud of his surname "O'Reilly", and made a clear cut distinction between the different factions of the Clan. "I am none of the Queen's O'Reilly" he boasted, "I'm a descendent of the Slasher who guarded the Bridge of Finea."

Cloakie thus proclaimed his descent from one of the chieftains who led the Breffni O'Reilly clan in the sixteen forty one rebellion. He was chiefly remembered for his penchant for the courts and it was said that he religiously saved three hundred pounds per annum to take his neighbours to court over any perceived slight or wrong.

Peter wrote on the road. It was his newspaper, his broadsheet (or should that be his longsheet), his campaigning pamphlet. From this pulpit he targeted all types of authority...Politicians, Courts, Judges, Councils and Corporations. They were all lampooned with equal generosity. He did not always see eye to eye with the local priest and both the latter and his housekeeper had unflattering cartoons of themselves painted on the roadway following a further falling out with Peter.

Eventually Peter passed to his final reward and was laid to rest by the same Padre in the church graveyard where the incursions of Peter's cattle had on many occasions raised the hackles of the Priest. However his sister arrived from America the day after the funeral and promptly declared that he was buried in a grave belonging to another family! Consternation ensued.

It was simply out of the question to approach the Priest, and a conclave of Undertaker, Grave digger and Church Warden or Caretakers decided to go ahead without his knowledge or consent and have an exhumation and reburial in the appropriate grave as quickly and surreptitiously as possible.

Well they started early in the morning and did the digging in both places but before they had filled in the now redundant grave, the Priest arrived taking an unexpected stroll. "Whats all the work then boys?" he enquired of his right hand man, the caretaker. "There's been a Resurrection" replied the latter.

The Priest came over and peered into the empty grave. "He's gone all right" he said. "Well he was trouble when he was above ground and now he's trouble when he's below ground" he declared without blinking an eyelid.

# 14

## *Unearthly Neighbours.*

Boy had we ghosts...we had them by the dozen.

It was said we owned the parish by day, but the ghosts and fairies and half forgotten deities owned it by night.

Their domain was delineated by the time of the day or more correctly the night. The darkness was the smokescreen under which they operated, but their powers were believed to be even more powerful under the soft moonlight - the friend and medium of love, magic and the unknown.

The area was littered with forts - concentric circular hills holding a commanding view of the surrounding countryside. These forts were the abodes, in fact the palaces of 'the good folk', 'the little folk', or as they were commonly known, the 'Fairies'.

The origin of these alternative dwellers has been disputed by historians and romantics and ignored by the population at large for decades, but the same population have not lost their belief in or their respect, mixed with a healthy dollop of fear for the 'Sidhe' as the Fairies are named in Gaelic.

Nobody but nobody, that I knew would plough or dig or interfere with a fairy fort. One man who had the audacity to plough an adjacent field to a particular fort found to his cost that his plough horse had died within a few months and he himself was afflicted with pains...a fate that was also the lot of anyone cutting down a lone whitethorn bush under the shadow of which was the Leprechaun's favourite resting place during the midday sun. The severe pains resulting from these 'sins' resembled (I am told) having a multitude of the trees thorns being pushed into your body - a la acupuncture.

The origins of the 'Sidhe' may be lost in the mists of time,

ALEC JOHNSTONS - LAIR OF THE
HEADLESS PIG.

but some solid foundation underpins the belief or it would not have lasted for thousands of years.

Their immediate presence in the area was a mixed blessing. They conferred good luck and health on the people who respected their abodes and customs and it was even rumoured that certain people, usually men, received even more special favours. The ladies of the Sidhe were reputed to be highly immoral in a sexual sense and it was believed that occasionally a man, often under the influence of John Barleycorn, John Jameson or Mr. Guinness would stand on a 'stray sod' and not be able to find his way home till morning. Some even related tales of being lured into the forts and spending hours or sometimes days in ecstasy with the Queen of the Sidhe, or one of her beautiful courtesans. However it is only fair to point out that a lot of women and particularly wives did not subscribe to the 'stray sod' theory.

Do ancient dramas, invasions or disasters inspire us to conjure up a supernatural icon or icons to help us overcome our fears, to ward off perceived evils or just help us in our daily battle to survive? Could contact with another civilization, possibly more advanced than ours, lead us to accord them extra natural powers? More likely our belief in the Sidhe stems from the folk memory of an invasion and struggle between the Celts or Milesians, and the Tuatha De Danaan and the subjugation of the latter or the silencing of their Religion, Priesthood and Gods by the new masters when their magic could not prevail against the iron swords and spears of the newcomers.

The fact that the 'Good Folk' reside in hill top forts is probably based on the fact that they made their last stands in these strong points.

The parish almost had dual religions. Christianity ruled supreme in the public domain but it had absorbed a multitude of beliefs and practices from the Older Religion. The sacred wells, trees, and feastdays had been taken over and given a Christian veneer, but underground there were yet still more beliefs which had never been assimilated or destroyed.

When our daytime lease ran out, the Older Gods reasserted their dominance stretching back long before recorded history and have obviously stood the test of time. Does an era

THE SENTINEL TREES, COVERED BY THE SACRED IVY,
GUARD THE ENTRANCE TO THE FAIRY FORT.

invoke its own deities ? Does the human psyche demand and create a deity specially tailored that it can implore to solve its problems and alleviate its tortures, but with a central continuous thread running through the belief system which acts as a kind of magnet attracting new bits and pieces throughout the centuries. Religions come and go but the lynchpin of all religions----the belief in some all powerful Being to whom we can turn for help survives for ever, and little bits of each belief system is adopted or attaches itself to the new or evolving belief and forms a link through our folklore that never dies.

We only have to look at our own parish.

Practically everyone went to the chapel on Sundays and also partook in Confessions, Baptisms, Marriages and Funerals - in fact in all the rituals of Christianity.

But we were also told and remembered the ghost stories, the fears and superstitions and good luck charms inherited from long before St. Patrick. Around the hearth, by the dim flickering light of the turf fire and the twin wick oil lamp, we listened hungrily to the ghostly sagas or happenings. Some of them were very relevant and real to us as each road from the house was guarded by one or more.

The Lady in White appeared along the Ardara lane, near the entrance to where a school once stood. Was she a former teacher coming back to impart her knowledge or maybe a pupil pining for unrequited love? And by the time you reached her stalking ground you had already run the gauntlet of the Fairy Fort. But it was no escape to turn left and go up Jim Mick's hill because in the 'gurteen' on your left, gaunt and lonely, stood the lone Whitethorn and who might be resting beneath it ?

You could of course turn right at the house and cycle into Bawnboy the back way, but along your route you would have to go past the ruins of John Dolans, Rocks and the Could Fellows, up the new line where the Black dog was seen, and not least the lair of the headless pig in Drumlougher. This creature came into existence, so the story went, because the farmer who lived there...Alec Johnston killed his pig on the 15th of August - a holy day, just to annoy his neighbours.

The stationary ghosts were bad enough but you could at

THE YEW TREE AT CASSIDYS CROSS. A
FEW HUNDRED YARDS FROM HERE "THE LADY IN
WHITE" WAS SAID TO APPEAR.

least have yourself psyched up or maybe send a quick message to your favourite saint when approaching their particular patch. But you also had to contend with the mobile variety, just like the modern customs patrols, in the guise of the Chain clanking man, the sow and bonhams, and the large Black Dog with red eyes. The last mentioned spectre patrolled the new line and followed Patrick O'Reilly (Hotcheen) home one night from a game of cards (25's), stopping when he stopped and following on after him when he resumed walking. Eventually Patrick threw him the cards, which scattered all over the lane and hurried into his house and locked the door.

When he awoke in the morning, the cards were neatly arranged on the crook hanging over the fire. The clergy themselves were not immune from these happenings, and I have heard on good authority that a priest called out at night to administer the last sacraments to a dying parishioner, would insist on being accompanied by another man.

Since the relentless onward march of electrification and the motor car, both of which are now universal, the harsh glare of artificial light has invaded the safe dark fastnesses of the ghostly domains and the sightings have become fewer. Is this the result of light clearing away our fears which were nurtured by the darkness or as one local wag pronounced "the so and so's who are around nowadays have frightened the ghosts away."

The area had the legends, Gods, Spirits and Demons that suited it at that time. The darkness of the countryside on the nights that the moon was at rest or clouds prevented her dreamy light from reaching us allowed our ghosts and demons to exist, roam and exercise their hold, but the relentless advance of 'civilization' - the cars, electric light and television have banished our fears and demons and then by necessity who needs Gods? The television has silenced our story tellers, our Seanachies, more effectively than foreign invaders or conquerors ever did and left us the poorer...a whole strata of folklore, belief and faith suddenly ripped away to leave a harsher, bleaker landscape of reality - a soulless environment of money-driven work necessary to survive.

The area may be dotted with ever more ostentatious houses and bungalows , and of course, people do deserve to live in

THE 'NEW LINE' — THE HAUNT OF THE
BLACK DOG WITH BLAZING RED EYES.

the best , but when the banks and money lenders get their cut at the end of each week or month is there the same appetite for neighbourliness, good humour and camaraderie around the hearth fire as there was in less progressive times?

# 15

## *Charms and Luck.*

Ghosts were one thing, but in a completely agricultural society at almost the same level of sophistication as that prevailing a thousand years ago, luck and charms were much more important.

Cattle and livestock were the mainstay of our economy, the yardstick of a mans wealth, and anything that interfered with their fertility or productivity was a serious matter indeed.

Churning butter was an area fraught with potential problems. Any neighbour or visitor coming into the house while the churning was in progress had to take a hand and help with the churning otherwise bad luck and consequently very little butter would be the result.

One time the dreaded thing did happen.

We had as usual collected basins full of cream which when ready were poured into a milk churn or creamery can which had been decked out with a tight fitting wooden lid, specially constructed for the job, with a hole in the middle through which a long handle had been inserted from the underside. A circular piece of wood had been nailed or screwed to the bottom of the handle. The actual churning consisted of pushing this up and down until the cream was churned and the butter collected on the top of the liquid or as it would be called at this stage, 'the buttermilk'.

Well we churned and churned, taking turns to rest our arms, but if we kept it up until we were blue in the face no butter appeared or collected. My parents were worried, especially my mother. Nobody had come into the house during the churning but nevertheless she believed that somebody had taken our luck. She insisted that Dad went up to Fr. Bradys with some salt which he would 'bless' and hours later after putting in the salt and churning again the butter collected in its usual abundance.

It is perhaps significant that both salt and a blessing were used in removing the 'spell', as salt has been a traditional guard against evil in many cultures.

Although I have always possessed a strong sense of scepticism, I am forced to admit that though I was both an observer and participant on that day, I have no answer to the churning enigma.

Your luck could be taken in many ways. The taker could achieve that by beating a hay rope against both sides of the mearning fence between you and them. If it was your cattle that was in their sights you might be able to defend your stock by tying a red ribbon on their horns to ward off the evil eye. Fairies were also believed to be able to steal your milk. My aunt assured me that neighbours sometimes heard a mothers voice coming from a fairy fort soothing a child and saying "It wont be long now untl milking time", and sure enough one of the cows would kick over and spill a bucket of milk.

The most novel way I heard of a farmer's cows' productivity being taken harked back to the days of witchcraft and shape changing. A Mister H...suddenly found that his cows produced only a fraction of their former daily output of milk. Having established that nothing was physically wrong with his animals he decided to literally ride shotgun on his herd and sat up all night keeping a lookout. During the night he noticed a hare moving from cow to cow in the meadow, suckling each in turn. He fired at the hare and wounded it before it escaped. The cows were soon back to their usual quota but a certain old lady - one of his neighbours - walked with a limp from then on.

To find a clutch of eggs or a joint of meat in the middle of one of your fields was a very bad sign and required immediate counter action to prevent disaster.

Some people were considered to be unlucky per se, without any malice aforethought, and thus the misfortunes attendant on their actions were usually spoken of in a jocular way. Michael Curran told me a story about a certain days poteen-making during the nineteen sixties on the local mountain. For those unfamiliar with the craft of distilling the heady spirit, the method is loosely as follows ;

You steep or put cut up fruit - say apples, pears or any other sweet fruit to hand in a large container of soft water, usually a creamery can and plenty (maybe a stone or two) of sugar. Cover with a cloth to protect but do not make it airtight. This mixture should have matured in about three to four weeks, and is called 'the wash'...and now the distilling process can commence.

This involves transferring the wash to preferably a copper cylinder - a central heating hot water cylinder is ideal - placed on top of a very hot but slow burning fire. It is then distilled off as steam through a copper pipe called a worm, coming from the top and winding round and round through a barrel of cold water to condense it back into a liquid in a collection vessel.

Well one chilly cold day two practicioners of the poteen art who had no desire to enlarge the Chancellors coffers were just about ready to distill 'the wash' in their still in an outhouse on one of the lanes or roads which led up towards the mountain. There was a patchwork of these, like the spokes of a wheel converging near the top, and the local postman, Ned Darcy, when delivering his letters would sometimes cross the intervening fields to avoid the longer journey up another lane.

Our distillers had the fire going strong and were getting on with the work when suddenly one of them espied a figure in uniform coming across the fields. "The Guards, The Guards" one cried out and the other one leapt into action to destroy the evidence and especially to quench the tell tale smoking fire. He reached out and grabbed a bucket which in his haste he thought was water and threw it on the fire. Alas the bucket contained not water but 'wash', which is extremely flammable, and the resulting explosion removed the roof of the outhouse to the complete astonishment of the postman who was merely delivering some government circular about the 'Warable Fly Eradication Scheme'! Ned was never likely to be regarded as the patron saint of the poteen trade from then on.

There could be a fusion of Christian and earlier rituals in keeping your luck. Half burned sticks or embers from the bonfire were thrown into crop fields. Cattle would be driven between two burning posts or driven clockwise like the sun around the bonfire. Depending on the day it took place it might seem that it was a particular Christian saint who was being asked to intercede on our behalf but in reality it was part of the old pagan rituals as exemplified by the feast days of Beltane, Lughnasa or maybe Samhain.

A friend told me about a woman who was reputed to possess 'powers'. She came out of her house and sprinkled holy water in a circle around a cow her husband had just sold to a neighbour. The buyer promptly refused to continue with the deal and insisted on having his money back. He was convinced that her actions were intended to insure that the worth of the animal would never leave their yard.

# 16

## *Legends.*

Some of the legends held out the promise of great material riches, providing all the parts fell into place. My aunt often told me the story of the pot of gold in the little garden near Thady's lane. This, I hasten to add, was not spoken of as a story, she and several others believed implicitly in it. It was buried in the small garden - actually a small meadow and you had to dream of it three nights in succession in order to have any chance of finding it.

Three men from Carrigallen did dream about it the necessary three nights on the trot and furthermore they were each informed in the dream about the other two. They saw the meadow or garden clearly, its location and the spot in it where the treasure was buried. The dreams were very specific - two were to do the digging, and one to hold the light...a hurricane lamp.

As is usual in Celtic folklore there was a geasa or strict condition which had to be observed - that is no one other than the three who had dreamed must be watching!

The men travelled from Carrigallen, making sure to arrive after dark and commenced digging. After half an hour their spades were striking the the metal casket. The noise awoke Mrs. Thady who came out of her house and peered through the bushes at the figures in the light of the lamp. The geasa had been broken, and although they dug desperately for hours and hours they could not find the casket again.

The other quest was also for gold - the metal that seems to have fascinated mankind as long as we have been on Earth. It concerned a Cromwellian or Elizabethan soldier who before he died is said to have hidden his gold in a ditch so that his neighbours would not find it. His actions or the rumours of them

MAGUIRES CHAIR. BELIEVED TO BE THE
TRADITIONAL NATURAL STONE THRONE WHERE
THE CHIEFS OF THE MAGUIRE CLAN
WERE INSTALLED.

prompted the same neighbours to great feats of endeavour to try and find it. Ditches were levelled, ponds drained and outhouses taken apart stone by stone, but the whereabouts of the fortune has remained a mystery, or maybe the finder was able to hold both his tongue and his liquor.

The gold fever still strikes from time to time, and an unexplained area of disturbed soil or the extra premium paid for a certain field when they come up for sale bears testimony to the potency of the stories and their ability to instil in a new generation of mens' hearts the craving for the yellow metal.

THE COTTAGE, WITH A HOLE BURNED IN THE
THATCH, WHERE THE 'DEVIL' FLEW OUT
FOLLOWING A CEREMONY TO EXORCISE HIM.

# 17

# *Outings.*

We had two main outings a year - one to Knock and one to Bundoran.

Knock is a village in County Mayo where at the site of the local church, the Blessed Virgin is said to have appeared to four local people in the Nineteen Twentys. The church has now grown to cathedral size and became firstly a destination for countrywide pilgrimages and lately for international pilgrims.

When my mother brought Enda, Father and myself - she was the prime mover - to Knock, it was experiencing a period of steady growth and was bursting at the seams with stalls selling religious items and icons and an ever expanding variety of other items mostly tasteless and tacky.

The names of all intending to travel to Knock on the coach had to be handed in to the priest several weeks before the travel date and our names were invariably in first. The excursions were always on a Sunday after the half past eight Mass. The preparations started early on a Saturday, shoes polished, trousers pressed, best hat taken out of its box for airing and off to bed early because the alarm clock would be set for the unearthly hour of five o'clock on Sunday morning.

Outing or not, pilgrimage or not, the farm livestock had to be seen to first and they were, because after all they were our bread and butter. So the clank of buckets and the steady zip zip of milk into them could be heard from shortly after five am. The whole house was a hive of activity and to cap it all there would be no breakfast because if you intended to receive Holy Communion then you had to abstain from food from twelve o'clock the night before. The only exception was Kwells tablets forcibly administered to ensure there was no travel sickness.

Now Dolly had to be caught by the lure of oats in a bucket and we set off in the trap to the chapel before eight. The horse was stalled in the arches underneath the chapel and fed and watered to last him throughout the day. The women who are nearly always the more religious, dominated the coach journey, asking whichever Priest was accompanying us to lead the Rosary. However there was one occasion when things didn't go according to their plans and Fr. Young spent his time telling us (the younger ones) jokes and conundrums much to the matriarchs dismay. Instead of the Rosary he had contests in which we had to repeat word tremblers- two that I recall were :-

> I saw a saw in Warsaw,
> And above all the saws
> I ever saw, the saw I saw,
> Was the best saw I ever saw,
> In Warsaw.

And when we managed to repeat that in the required few seconds he then changed to :-

> I went into a felt hat shop
> And felt a felt hat,
> And above all the felt hats
> I ever felt,
> The felt hat I felt,
> Was the best felt hat
> I ever felt,
> In a felt hat shop.

The men came into their own during our halfway stop in Elphin when a sizable number of Guinnesses and hot whiskies with a Port for the ladies and lemonade for us youngsters were consumed in record time. On my first trip I was given a big brown threepenny bit and I thought I was a millionaire.

We may have been on a pilgrimage but we didn't neglect the 'day out' aspect of the trip and made hay while the sun shone, so after the religious activities were over we repaired to a restaurant or eating house and indulged ourselves to a 'meat tea' with all the trimmings, and I am sure the men must have managed a few pints more than we were aware of because quite a symphony of snores disturbed our rest throughout the eighty miles to home. Bundoran was a different kettle of fish.

If Knock was the Fatima of our world then Bundoran was the Las Vegas. Nearly all the young people of the Parish took part in the outing to Bundoran. It was the highlight of the year and we gave it our all.

My Father gave me a pound and I used to help Pee Ned at turf on the Saturday, the day before the trip and he gave me ten shillings which meant I had a magnificent thirty shillings in total, enough for all the excesses I hoped to encounter. For all the boys and girls courting it was a great opportunity to get away from Parents, relatives and prying eyes and for the rest on the lookout the prospect of success in the new arena was intensified. The coach started off at about eleven as the journey to Bundoran was only fifty miles compared to the eighty to Knock, and we sang all the way up through Glangevlin, past the Shannon Pot and through the forest drive.

The road took us past majestic Ben Bulben - the bald mountain and close by Lough Gill, immortalised by W.B.Yeats before reaching Bundoran, our nearest seaside resort.

Seven of us, all boys, made the Breffni eating rooms our first port of call, and not having yet developed a haute cuisine taste, we ordered mashed potato, ham and peas SEVEN TIMES!

The one arm bandits and the bumping cars at the corner of the beach road were a great attraction. They were only a few yards from the Bargain Kings pitch and we were fascinated by his sales patter and his ability to keep an armful of plates in the air at the same time. He had an uncanny ability to keep a crowd enthralled and shame his audience into buying - "This crowd here are obviously from the poorhouse. If all the rest were like you I'd be in the poorhouse myself." We always ended up buying a trinket or two - a Swiss army knife, a globe encasing a snowstorm or a plate with 'Our Home' painted on it.

Bundoran had a couple of beaches, but we were not

BUNDORAN. WITH THE CLIFFS AND SEA ON
THE LEFT THE ROAD LED TO 'THE FAIRY
BRIDGES' -- A POPULAR COURTING SPOT.

swimming people and were not inclined to spend our special day in water when the elements poured enough of it on us when we were at home.

The courting couples made their way to the Fairy bridges, out among the sand dunes, but us young bucks were keeping our energies and hopes for the Astoria Ballroom that night. We believed or more likely hoped that all holidaymakers and especially tourists from abroad were immoral hedonists and prayed that those in the Astoria would not have discovered virtue and the saving grace was if you did make a complete idiot of yourself well at least you were far from home.

One of the top showbands, the Melody Aces, were playing the venue that night and with about two thousand patrons packed in our fantasies were given full rein and our earlier prayers were answered! We were under strict instructions to be back by eleven pm, but the crack was just too good and we dragged it out till two in the morning. The older members were already fast asleep on the coach when we made our appearance, and the organiser Pee Francis vowed we would never be brought on the outing again...but come next year the need to make up the numbers secured us a 'last chance'.

Coaches were the means of transport to Knock and Bundoran. The horse and trap brought us to Corlough but the bicycle was the individuals means of transport and the liberator par excellence. Once mastered it was never forgotten, it was practically maintenance free as tyres, bald or not not were still tyres to us and even the tubes lasted a lifetime or as long as the repair patches could find a solid grip on them.

Our first bike was a mongrelised version put together by Frank and Fr. Greg McGovern. It was a mans bicycle, that is it had a cross bar, and it would shake the life out of you as it had no inner tube on either wheel. Instead they had managed to put two tyres on each wheel so punctures were not likely to be a problem. Brakes were another luxury it did not possess, and we slowed down by rubbing our heel against the tyre of the back wheel. We all learned to ride on that bicycle and even when we were too small to sit on the saddle or ride over the bar, we managed to navigate with one leg under the bar to reach the far pedal in a convoluted figure of eight.

The cycle machine opened up the possibility of rapid journeys beyond our normal range, and when equipped with the flashlamp brought the first vestiges of light to our darkened laneways during the nights' meanderings. My father told me of the time when a neighbour bought the first carbide lamp, the battery flashlamp's predecessor, in Ballinamore at the end of a fair day. The merchant lit it up, fixed it on the bicycle, and sent him on his way. Everything was hunky dory on the journey but on reaching home he couldn't turn it off and sat up with it all night in case it would burn the house down.

There is one other blessing that the bicycle never gets credit for. During the time when it reigned supreme, it enabled the youth to venture far out of their little home areas in search of a mate, and quite probably helped to diversify the gene pool. Would some boffin conduct a survey, with the aid of a grant from Brussels to see if this development had any bearing on the explosion in IT geniuses and the creation of the Celtic Tiger in later years.

# 18

## *Border Humour.*

The border loomed large in all our lives and generated its own dark brand of gallows humour. Sean O'Heslin, after whom the football pitch in Ballinamore is named was a Republican, a Teacher and an admirer of beautiful women. He also had a fondness for the drink. One day he was enjoying a quiet drink in Bawnboy, when his reverie was interrupted by a stranger who had obviously enjoyed a few drops himself. The newcomer went on to wreak his venom on an absent soul...the Pope. Sean, after much restraint, grabbed him by the throat whils't enquiring menancingly "What have you got to say about the Pope now?" "Nothing." replied his adversary, "But he's got a damn bad name around Portadown."

On a lighter note there was the story of the mother and daughter who go into the local store. The daughter is getting plumper by the day in a maternal sort of way, and the store owner remarks on this. "She's been stung by a bee" the mother explains hurriedly. "It must have been a bee special" replies the store owner, alluding to the unlamented auxiliary police force who often patrolled in the North.

The local drinking rhyme embraced both sides of the Border:

'Ballinamore ---the dirty hole,
Swanlinbar the dandy,
Lisnaskea for drinking tay,
And Maguire's bridge for brandy'.

# 19

## *And The Yankees Came...*

Millions of Irish emigrated to the Americas-especially the United States and Canada. They retained a very strong affection for the Emerald Isle...and for the relatives, friends and neighbours they left behind. Their triumphs and disasters were relayed to home and the news from home flowed westward as well.

A Kerryman told me how a family from near his home went on a holiday to New York, and on the obligatory trip down Fifth Avenue they met former neighbours from Kerry who had emigrated generations before, "So hello said we to they, and hello said they to we." Fortunately most meetings produced a lot more talk and banter than that - perhaps both these groups were teetotal! Occasionally the emigrants, their children or grandchildren would return to look up their roots.

In the sixties, some far out relatives of ours who were also related to Patrick O'Reilly arrived from Florida - a mother and daughter, neither of whom had ever been to Ireland before. Patrick who had never previously travelled further from home than Ballybay in the neighbouring county of Monaghan, hired a hackney car and went down to Shannon airport to meet their flight, and after many hours he arrived back in Corlough, accompanied by his niece and grand niece.

They stopped at our house first and in accordance with tradition were invited in for something to eat - cooked ham, tomatoes and bread and tea...a 'mate tay', as we called it. During the meal, Father and Enda arrived in from the meadow where they had been working at the hay. All the greetings were exchanged, hugs of welcome given and received and the food consumed.

My mother, a righteous, God-fearing woman who never

even mentioned the word bum, inquired of the teenager what her favourite pastimes were, to be answered without hesitation "Tennis and Sex". Enda, to whom I am indebted for this information, nearly exploded but was under the impression that my mother did not fully understand the Florida twang.

The grand niece's indiscretions did not end there, albeit the next one was unintentional. In those days most country houses did not have running water so consequently there were no toilets or bathrooms. After the meal, when Mary Lou (I do not remember her real name) announced that she was going to have a shower, Patrick tried to diffuse the situation by replying "Well the only shower you're likely to get here will be in the meadow referring to mother's nature well known penchant of pouring water on our efforts to dry the hay. Mary Lou hadn't a clue what he was on about and reiterated her intention to douse her tired limbs with some of our ample rainfall, so Patrick, never one to shirk his duty, now had to be quite blunt "Don't you know, young lady that houses in this area don't have those kind of facilities." Mademoiselle digested this awful fact and, summing up the reserves of all her determination to survive outside of air conditioned indulgence, declared "That's OK...I'll have a bath instead"!

There must have been deep currents of anxiety coursing through their minds as the car, carrying the two of them and Patrick, wound its way along the bog road up to Patrick's abode and through the gates, adorned with a cow's head on each pier to ward off evil spirits and bad luck. Cathy greeted them at the doorway and extended a warm welcome, but then must have put the fear of God into them by exclaiming, whilst showing them their bedroom "You'll be sleeping in here but you'll have to piss outside."

One can only surmise what terrified whispers were exchanged between the two visitors during the dark night in that lonely landscape before blessed sleep arrived, but two tearful tourists hurried along the lane in the morning to request Enda to drive them into the pale of civilization. Numerous mugs of tea and the passing of several hours calmed their anxieties, but perhaps the most delicate point was in ensuring that from now on, they would be able to recognise and avoid nettles as these herbs had caused them not a little pain that very morning. You see, when performing the essential cleansing rites post toilette in the paddock, our intrepid American adventurers had utilised the nettles, rather than the grass the natives would have plucked in a similar situation.

After a few days the visitors got into the hang of things, hired a car and managed to excite the local males by availing of a week of good weather to sport that year's top fashion hit...matching red hot pants. This of course didn't fall in line with Patrick and Cathy's idea of propriety. Nor did their habit of arriving home at three or four in the morning from some hard rock dances, or by asking why was he playing with the grass as he won the hay, nor indeed did an overlong visit by the fire brigade to rescue their car from a gravel hole...but they developed a liking and respect for each other despite cultural shocks on both sides, and they came back for a further visit the following year.

When we were young, Yankees and visitors in general always seemed to arrive when the house was in turmoil, with sheets of 'The Anglo Celt' on the floor, and the walls being whitwashed with lime. Mum would be mortified, but after a while one of us would be despatched to Cassidys or Feehans for a Swiss role with strict instructions to put it in the back window and not show that we hadn't already got a cake in the house when they arrived, tea would be made and all the relatives avidly discussed.

One couple arrived, and as luck would have it, James Eddie came in at the same time. This was most fortunate as he would be able to remember more of the old days. James duly did his bit, but one quirk of his did cause a few eyebrows to rise a bit. When referring to the era when he was more youthful and vigorous, he always said "When I was alive" and my relative's beautiful wife, a former dancer on Broadway wondered whether he was fully flesh and bone.

The missionary who arrived one day was not an American, nor a returning Irishman but a Jehovah Witness from Czechoslovakia. How on earth he ended up in our neck of the woods must remain one of the greatest navigational mysteries of the century. He tried to convert my brother, but seeing that his seed was falling on barren ground, he turned his attention to

James. "We get enough of that every Sunday in Corlough" replied James, "But I'll tell you one thing, you're a very silly man to come up that bad lane in your good car". He was never seen again.

## 20

## *The attack on Arcadia.*

Forces outside our control were conspiring to destroy our Arcadia. The first blow was a deadly dagger disguised as a carrot. "It will make your life so much easier" was its mantra. You should always beware 'Greeks bearing gifts'. The electricity was coming.

Meetings were held to decide whether the Parish would accept it at all. But there was never any doubt. The blandishments of the advertisers were as ever directed strongly towards the fairer sex. The electric pylons were fanning out like the castles of a conquering Norman army. Our mountains, lakes and bogs which had successfully resisted the advance of the actual Norman invaders, and their successors hundreds of years before were of no avail this time. "The electric light will be brighter" true, "It wont be smelly like paraffin", "It will be quick, available at the press of a button" true, all true. The cost - this was not mentioned in the adverts and when brought up, was dismissed with a patronizing half sneer - 'a fraction of a penny per unit', which meant nothing.

The juggernaut could not be stopped. The wiring was installed, the bulbs switched on and the Tilley lamps became redundant, and were soon hidden from view and forgotten, covered by cobwebs amongst the rafters in the barns.

The arrival of the electricity was a hammer in the nail of the coffin of self-sufficiency, and a debt free existence. Within a week a sharp suited salesman from Dublin was knocking on the door with an absolutely great offer 'that could never be repeated' on an electric cooker. "It's a marvellous offer, at barely cost because we are selling so many. All your neighbours are having one, and the great thing about electricity is that the more you use, the less it costs you per unit" the suited one jabbered on. "Do you mean to say that the more I use the less I will have to pay?" enquired my father. Mr. Suit left, but it was only a temporary reprieve. The damage had been done. The very fact that the installation had been completed meant that the salesman had a permanent foot in the door.

The Wet and Dry battery radio soon followed the Tilley lamps, and was replaced by an electric radio. The genie had been released from the bottle and its tentacles were getting longer and longer.

It had spread its brightness to the cow byre and the yards. The bills, tiny at first, were a little larger now, but the bait had been swallowed and could not be disgorged. The demon now opened the doors to all types of creatures with voracious appetites; cookers, fires, fridges, televisions and tape recorders. And these creatures were not 'inanimate'. No, they gave birth or spawned new creations at a frightening pace. Microwaves, videos and the like who all proceeded to feed on the corpse of the independent, self-sufficient smallholder and not in one way but several...first by buying the appliance, secondly by repairing them when necessary and thirdly paying the continual cost of running them.

The capital cost of acquiring the electric goodies was in itself considerable for a community with limited disposable cash, but the insidious legacy was the quarterly bill with the vile standing charges, the most annoying of all pounds of flesh which these corporate vampires are now licensed to take from our very breasts.

At the same time as the invasion of the Pylons, the enemy opened up a second front...tractors were pushed into the fray against our beloved horses.

The horse has held a fascination for the Celts since time immemorial. The evidence can be seen in the beautiful artefacts in wood and precious metals from the La Tene and Hallstadt areas of Celtic culture and habitation. This is hardly a surprise when you consider that the Celts evolved on the southern steppes of eastern Europe and Asia Minor, where the horse was essential in those enormous plains bounded only by ever more distant horizons. The horse was the transport and the battering tank of these reckless warriors on their forays throughout Anatolia, Egypt, Northern

Europe, Italy and into Greece where they sacked Delphi. The Celts were a westward moving people, and this special animal must have proved its worth a millionfold in the migration and numberless raids and battles all the way to the Atlantic wall of the west of Ireland. The horse had never lost its mystique for the Celt, whether it was the long legged thoroughbred racehorse, hardy Connemara pony or powerful warhorse or workhorse, and the respect between man and horse never wavered - till now.

The blandishments were quite similar to those of the electricity companies - the tractor was the thing of the future. It was much more powerful, it was quicker...the more go-ahead farmers everywhere were using it - in the States, Britain, Continental Europe and even in the more advanced areas of Ireland. Who were we to stand in the way? The price was enormous compared to a horse, but of course our friendly dealers had the most generous terms...a small deposit and regular small payments. As the words of the ode to hire purchase went;

"You can have anything you seek,
For a dollar down and a dollar a week."

Except it wasn't a dollar...it was many pounds, and the noose of indebtedness was tightened another notch tighter around the necks of freemen.

The tractor needed regular feeding on diesel and oil-the free grass that the horse had enjoyed did not figure in its diet. It needed frequent servicing, and it had another major fault - it did not reproduce itself. So another stack of notes had to be found and another debt incurred when its heir and replacement were born.

Dolly still provided the power to transport us in the trap to mass on Sundays, but even here his tenure was under threat. The metal progeny of Henry Ford was spreading out in concentric circles from the major towns, and Prefects and Populars were appearing in even the remotest areas, and daring to park where the horses traps once held pride of place. Another Capital bill had arrived - quite a hefty one at that, and it had its three acolyte bills in attendance...tax, insurance and a weekly one for petrol.

Governments of all shades encouraged this development. Perhaps we should bring a case for premeditated entrapment, as they clearly saw that their future lifeblood of taxation was going to flow from these little toys, and the tax did indeed flow and has continued to this present day, starting as little streams and growing to mighty rivers of Amazonian proportions.

The need to have more and more cash to pay for all this increased expenditure was becoming more and more paramount - a complete break with the ways of the past was a vital necessity as the old way of farming with self sufficiency at its core and a little left over from the sale of milk and calves was not enough anymore. Specialisation was the name of the game, and the commissars of the revolution were the agricultural advisors. They were eagerly preaching the gospel of the new era and its sacraments were slatted houses, feeding areas, marshalling areas, silage pits and milking parlours, plus all the machinery to go with them.

The advisers were the apostles of this process. After all there would be no point in having them and paying their salaries if things were to remain the same. Their enthusiasm knew no bounds and they became indistinguishable from the fertiliser and other salesmen whose company cars now beat a regular path to the farmer's door.

The farmers themselves now had a new and frequent pilgrimage to make to the local shrine of moneylending - the bank. Words like business profiles, cash flow projections and increased yields sprouted like weeds. The carefree days were numbered. There was no longer any time for convivial chats in front of the blazing hearth fire in the evenings in this profit and loss society. In fact, the blazing hearth fires were disappearing like snowflakes in June to be replaced by shiny new cookers.

Needless to say the people did not embark on these massive changes without some carrot, and carrots in plenty were produced and dangled invitingly in front of their intended victims. Like the claymores or battleaxes of old, the attack was two edged. The indoor goodies were aimed at the housewife - electricity, cookers, radios, cleanliness, comfort and the outdoor goodies needed to generate the necessary income to afford them the tractors, slatted houses, silage pits et al had to be bought at any cost by their husbands. And oh yes...an increase in the price of milk was given, and the advisers were loud in their proclamations that an ever increasing quantity would be needed to satisfy the demand for the new value added products such as cheese, dried milk and chocolate powder, but they always insisted that the new regulations were going to be very strict and only those farmers with the top facilities, the slatted houses, running water and all the rest on the list would be able to partake of this bonanza... "the rest will be left behind-their places will not pass the inspectors".

The division had started. Now, if you were not large enough to support the modernisation, there were only two alternatives. Acquire more land if you were able to, and could raise the loan and find a suitable farm near you to buy, or go out of milk production altogether. So another carrot was provided to entice people to forsake their right to supply milk to the creamery, which had been theirs since the co-operative movement was founded. A subsidy was paid to any farmer who suckled their calves on the cows and ceased dairying.

Beef production was completely new to these small farmers and, in the opinion of many and especially with hindsight, unsuitable. Small hill farms were now competing with the ranch style holding of the central plain, and with the massive farms of England, America, Australia and Argentina. It was a classic David and Goliath situation, only in this case it doesn't need much imagination to figure out who will dominate when a level playing field is introduced and subsidies are withdrawn as they inevitably will.

Those who opted to remain in Dairying were now entering a very different world from that which we had enjoyed. The days when we cut the hay with the horse and machine were gone. There was to be no more beautiful Summer days tedding it with a pitchfork, lapping it, building handshakings or cocks, or tying them down with hay ropes made with the winder. No more would we sit down at the base of the cocks and drink our tea or buttermilk from the gallon can from which we might have had to expel some leaping young frogs. No those days were disappearing like Autumn leaves in the fairy whirlwinds.

Silage was now to be the cattle's main winter food - a foul replacement for the beautiful honey-scented, well won hay. It should be pointed out that fluid from silage, if it escapes into a river or stream, will kill all fish life in the area it pollutes. This same fluid in the moist silage is digested by the cattle and helps form the milk, dairy products and beef, which constitute a major part of our food intake. Is all well that remains hidden? Does the danger evaporate if the medical authorities and their bosses the politicians ignore it. Future generations may regret the nonchalance with which this subject is treated, but as usual 'nobody' will be responsible.

The meadows now looked completely different after the mowing. The silage was drawn in immediately and deposited in a pit or heap, some molasses were poured through it to make it palatable; it was covered with a large plastic sheet and weighed down with old tyres to exclude the air. The cows were no longer fed in their individual or twin compartments, but required to eat through the apertures in a gate slung across the entrance to the silage pit.

To an observer it would seem that the powers that be had launched a concentrated effort to depopulate the countryside and group all the people closely together in cities, towns and villages where they can keep an eye on them. New quotas were introduced on the total volume of milk a creamery could accept, and they in turn passed the quota down to their individual suppliers. Now instead of the endless demand for milk that the advisors had been loudly proclaiming a few years earlier, penalties would be levied on any farmer producing more than his allocation.

The beef farmers had also received a less than welcome new directive...many had kept Friesian cows whom they crossed with the beef Charolais bulls as Charolais command a higher price as beef animals. They would buy another calf from a Dairy farmer and suckle both on a Friesian cow as they generated more milk. "You can no longer do that" intoned the government bosses. "Only a Charolais calf can be suckled on a Charolais cow and the beef farmer can no longer keep Friesian cows." Naturally the government pays out less subsidy and the farmer has a smaller income.

All these developments reduced the population of our area in a dreadful manner, but our leaders were still not satisfied. They had another device up their sleeve ready to unleash. As usual it was going to be of immense benefit, the answer to our dreams and

135

provide the elusive jobs. It did nothing of the sort. The new menace could nearly be equated with the Roman revenge on Carthage after they defeated that state at the battle of Zama and ploughed salt into the land to ensure that it was rendered completely unfertile. The menace was and is 'The Silent Enemy'... the Forestry programme.

The Celts we are told, when they came to Ireland, cleared the forests to make agriculture possible and allow the people to till the soil and settle the land. Many large and happy families were raised on those small farms. Crime was non existent, community spirit was extremely strong and the old, the infirm or the unfortunate were looked after by their neighbours, as Thomas Gray wrote;

"Oft did the harvest to their sickle yield;
Their furrow oft the stubborn glebe has broke.
How jocund did they drive their team afield;
How bow'd the woods beneath their sturdy stroke."

Well the Forestry commission has reversed the settlement of thousands of years. They have taken these small farms and indeed much larger ones as well, which they are pleased to call 'marginal', and planted their ubiquitous pines at every opportunity. Nobody, the writer included, would mind if they confined their planting to places where the people had been unable to till or graze, but dammit maybe I would still care because they are changing the environment willy-nilly without consideration, destroying the habitat of the grouse and goodness knows how many other species, and poisoning the mountain trout streams.

And the promised carrot? The jobs? Where are they? What became of them? Where are the paper mills and sawmills? Well they certainly didn't come to our neck of the woods. In fact they didn't come to Ireland at all. No, a new development enables one or two men in a single day to cut and load the specially equipped lorry which speeds to the nearest port and pronto, our bastard pines joins its cousins once removed in Scandinavia where they are compressed into paper to print the kind of magazines which would make your Granny's hair or maybe even your own stand on your head. But even that is not the end...they leave the roots and base of each tree behind so that the area resembles nothing more than a lunar landscape that has somehow managed to sprout regular lines of enormous flat mushrooms.

The forestry plantations gets it's 'Silent Enemy' title from the effect that they have on neighbouring farms. Nobody likes having one of them adjoining their land. Crops do not flourish next to them, the ground does not dry properly as it is shielded from the drying effect of the wind, and most important of all it cuts off a farmer from contact with his neighbours...and that is devastating to a social people like the Celts.

The small, independent, self-sufficient freemen have no natural allies in the present political set up. Granted there are politicians who genuinely care about their survival and do try to help, but the juggernaut wheels of authority keep on turning and each new regulation and directive is another nail in the proverbial coffin.

The centre and rightest parties both cull favour from large farmers, big business and professional people. The left wingers look after the interests of unionised labour, and have a natural antipathy to these nonconformist tillers of the soil akin to that of Stalin toward the Gulags, and do not seem to suffer any traumas over their demise. The left were the earliest advocates of intensive forestry as the new raw material for the country - less imports and more jobs - but instead it has brought a gloom of lifeless solitude to areas formerly buoyant with men and animals, living out a life of co-existence as old as civilization.

The authorities always had a problem with our type of area. We had not been entered on the lists of hire purchase agencies, and we did not figure on bankers' files. We paid no National Insurance, our names did not pop up in the concertina files of the Tax gatherers. We did not frequent doctors or vets, and having no cars, the national register could not identify us. In fact if any busybody department had a file labelled Corlough, then it is highly unlikely that there was anything inside it. This is a most happy arrangement for those whose names do not appear, but it is the original bureaucratic nightmare.

An empty file to a bureaucrat is like a treeless riverbank to a beaver.

So by hook or by crook, this situation has got to be changed. The people must be counted, listed in alphabetical order, surnames first and all and any little tittle-tattle added.

The first attempts at comprehensive record keeping took place at the introduction of the old age pension before the foundation of the state in the early nineteen hundreds. People couldn't believe that a government whose predecessors for over seven hundred years had tried to kill them, steal their lands and animals, persecute their language and religion, were going to give them something for nothing. Of course first lists had to be made, ages ascertained and verified - not as simple as it might seem. Many people had not been registered. After all they felt that the government and administration were not of their choosing so why register.

Now, many long (or should I say ancient) tales of longevity were concocted. Could you remember certain great storms, severe flooding, heavy snow lasting for very long periods? Or maybe political events or maybe a battle or two? Any of these could have a decisive effect on whether or not you became the weekly recipient of the sum of five shillings. I bet it was introduced shortly before an election. But though they probably gave it scant thought at the time, the compilation process had begun. Lists were being made and now it was in your interest to have your details properly recorded so that when walking stick time arrived, there would be no need to strain aged brain cells to try and pretend that you remembered massive storms or scandals of nearly seventy years ago.

I remember the guards calling to make the census of the livestock and fowl, and check to see if the gun and dog were licensed. Naturally he was told a bundle of lies and given a whiskey or two to ensure that he didn't become too officious. Twelve cows became seven, ten calves were five and hens, ducks, geese and turkeys became a mere fraction of themselves. If a dog (most families had two) could be spirited away for an hour or two, then no license would carry his name in the coming year. There was no obvious advantage in having the correct number of livestock entered on the census forms and this was coupled with a healthy belief "that they shouldn't be told everything".

In our young days, the mountain sheep farmers were nearly immune from the prying eyes and the pen and paper of the inquisitors. They could tell the guards or any other inspectors anything they wished, as it could not possibly be checked. The sheep roamed the mountains and did not respect the artificial border between North and South. Hardy men looked after them, sometimes travelling for days on foot, with their regulation two border collies for companions. They scoured hill and dale, counting their flock but not for the inquisitors, the latter had to be content with the numbers supplied to them. The lambs and wool might be sold in many different fairs in several counties on either side of the border. And cash was king, cheques being definitely Persona Non Grata.

One man told me of a visit he had from a tax inspector. He told the inspector that he had one hundred and fifty hens but Mr. Unbeliever insisted on checking for himself. The man handed the inspector the keys to the hen house at the end of a long and very wet field. He set off but arrived back a few minutes later with his shiny patent shoes covered in mud and other unmentionables, and most of his legs as well. Now, he asked to borrow a pair of Wellingtons and off he went again. The second time he came back, up to an hour later, he looked very unhappy and exclaimed, "they wouldn't stand still!"

The inquisitors have at last gathered the mountainy men into their net, and as usual the bait was filthy lucre. A subsidy was offered for each ewe and lamb. It was too good to miss. The forms were filled and the state suddenly realized its citizens possessed four or five times as many sheep as before. Some even borrowed animals from their Northern neighbours to substantiate their figures when the inspectors checked them at the local dipping stations. The subsidies were OK'd. There was much delight and winking at each other and celebration about how they had outwitted the inspectors and the scene was repeated some time later when the big cheque arrived.

But who had been outwitted? The joy became muted the following year when a retrospective tax demand arrived where none had been levied before and by the way next years application form had a new box which had to be filled in, it read "Tax assessment number".

Now the free inhabitants of the valleys and hills under the Cuilcagh mountains had been assessed, collated and entered in the computer.

How many databases are they now on? As one computer talks to another and a mail order concern attempts to corner more of the market, or insurance companies or other financial organisations pour out their literature to their selected targeting base - details they have acquired by buying census returns which we are forced to supply...the list gets bigger and bigger. Perhaps the most galling aspect of it all is that all this junk mail is printed on paper manufactured from the pines with which the forestry authorities have driven out the neighbours of the people receiving the letters!

Where now are the descendents of the households who have ceased to exist. They are scattered over the globe. Some have prospered, or as people would say "done well". Others have not done as well. Undoubtedly there are hearts longing to turn the clock back and immerse themselves in the certainty of the seasons, the rain, the frost, the crops, the flowers...

> "Had I the chance to wander back,
> Or own a kings abode,
> It's soon I'd see the hawthorn tree,
> Down the old bog road."

Of course nobody can deny that people have a right to change their ways, lifestyles, location and anything else they wish...in fact the God-given right to go to hell in their own way. But, and it is a very big but, they should be given a full and complete education concerning where certain choices will possibly lead them. Did anyone ever tell a man before he sold his farm to the Forestry that his grandchildren could end up in tenement flats in London or New York. Does anybody, teacher, preacher, lecturer or career adviser really 'A D V I S E' ? In mine and most people's experience, it goes something like "Oh yes Brady...radio operator on a ship, very good", "Smith...what's this I hear about you and journalism? Well if your essays are anything to go by, there'll be no

Nobel prize for literature!", "And Cullen. Well Cullen, what will become of you? Well, I don't care, I'll still have my pension!" I am being a bit flippant now, but the point I'm making is that what passes for career guidance is not 'guidance for a fulfilled life'. Depending on the particular career adviser, you may have a few words spoken to you in a superficial way, or they may drone on and on about various jobs or types of work, but nobody discusses the prospect of happiness in the future. Nobody tells you that it doesn't really matter how much you earn as the cost of your lifestyle will expand to eat up any earnings you may acquire.

If as a family you earn fifty thousand a year, your expenses - mortgage, cars, insurance, holidays and everything else needed to keep one step ahead of the Jones's will eat up that fifty thousand. The same will be true if you earn one hundred thousand, only the house will be bigger and so will the mortgage to pay for it...the cars will cost more and so will the holidays and clothes. The one hundred thousand family will be no better off than the smallholder of forty years ago. In fact it is likely that they will actually be worse off, and the pressures on them will be incomparable.

This scenario is undoubtedly widespread as we continue to 'progress', but its effects can be more readily seen in the context of the move from self-sufficiency to the rat race of the Global economy.

# 21

## *Arcadia Regained.*

What will the future hold for the regions under the Cuilcagh mountains and similar areas throughout the country and indeed the World? One thing is for sure...no particular system lasts forever, and eventually everything turns full circle. People are beginning to question the benefits of the madcap scramble for year on year growth and so-called progress. It is in the end unsustainable. The pressures on the young workers to create more and more wealth to pay for the pensions and medicines for an older population mean they are getting burned out at an early age.

But already there are signs that the cycle is turning. Industry has provided jobs, but the people are holding on to their land and the children of people who had moved to the towns and cities are clamouring to be allowed to build homes back in the open spaces where their ancestors once lived. This is heresy to the planners and officials who want to continue to herd them within town boundaries and leave the land clear so that on their weekends off they can cycle along and enjoy a human and house free view.

To verify this, witness the planning regulations and the objections to applications by the so-called heritage organisation who managed to object to every proposed rural house last year, and at the very last minute as well, in order to cause as much trouble as possible.

But the call of the countryside will not wane or fade. Crafts and arts groups are springing into life. Some wither and die but others survive and step-by-step, life is returning to the hills and the valleys. A wise man who had made the study of ancient Egypt his life long work once told me that the Egyptian gods only lost their power when people no longer called on their names.

I know what he meant...

We must not allow the beauty and indeed the hardships of a former way of life to be forgotten. The ghost stories, the ceilidhes, the sports, the simple way of earning a living must not be forgotten. Our holy wells, whitethorn trees and the fairy forts, the resting places and homes of the sidhe must not be erased from our collective folk memory, and go the way of the Egyptian gods. No ! Make sure to tell your children and grandchildren about them. Then our rich and vibrant folk memory and the area that gave it birth will continue to call to your bloodline wherever in the world you lay your weary head. The call will come and some of your descendents will make the long journey, enjoy the delights, the feeling of belonging, and even replant the genes in **the land below the mountains.**

**Would you like to re-establish
Links with the Celtic Essence ?**

Join

# THE CELTIC MYSTICAL UNION

*Special joining fee with this voucher*

Sterling £30
US $55
45 Euros
Regular updates from the Union
Fantastic cheap holidays in Ireland
Incorporating courses in Celtic Mysticism
and culture.
Commencing in 2006.
Earliest members get priority.

Celtic Mystical Union,
142 Devonshire Way,
Shirley, Croydon ,Surrey, CR0 8BT.
England.

And

Munlough, Bawnboy,
Co.Cavan.
Eire.

Next book by the Author:

# "THE COUSINS"

*A STORY OF LOVE, INTRIGUE, REBELLION*

*AND BETRAYAL, SET IN MODERN IRELAND*

*AND BRITAIN.*

BrightKing Publications
142 Devonshire Way
Shirley,
Croydon , Surrey CR08BT.

*And*

Munlough, Bawnboy,
Co.Cavan,
Eire.